CW00410142

hamlyn cookery club

More than
chicken

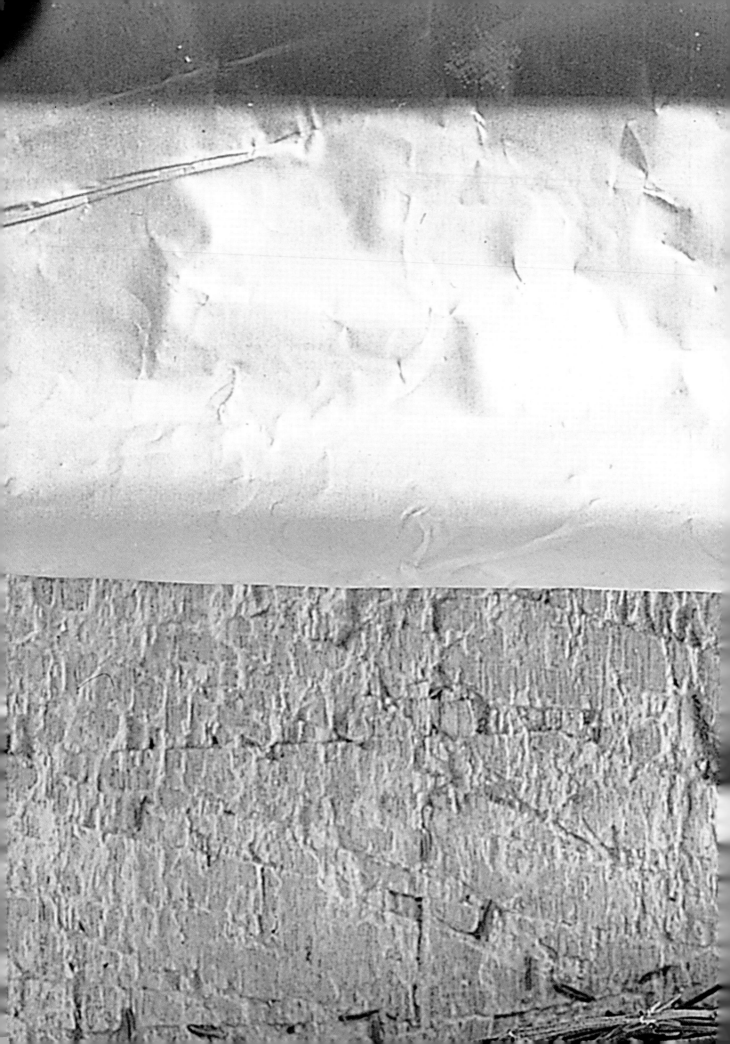

hamlyn cookery club

More than
chicken

First published in 1999 by Hamlyn
an imprint of Octopus Publishing Group Ltd
2–4 Heron Quays
London E14 4JP

Copyright © 1999 Octopus Publishing Group Ltd
All Photography Copyright © 1999 Octopus Publishing Group Ltd

All rights reserved. No part of this publication may be
reproduced, stored in a retrieval system, or transmitted, in any
form or by any means, electronic, electrostatic, magnetic tape,
mechanical, photocopying, recording or otherwise without the
prior written permission of the publisher.

British Library Cataloguing-in-Publication Data
A catalogue record for this book is available from the
British library.

ISBN 0 600 59916 7

Printed in China

Publishing Director: Laura Bamford
Copy Editor: Heather Thomas
Creative Director: Keith Martin
Design Manager: Bryan Dunn
Designer: Jo Tapper
Jacket Photography: Sean Myers
Picture Researcher: Christine Junemann
Senior Production Controller: Katherine Hockley

Notes

1 Both metric and imperial measurements have been given in all recipes. Use one set of measurements only and not a mixture of both.

2 Standard level spoon measurements are used in all recipes.
1 tablespoon = one 15 ml spoon
1 teaspoon = one 5 ml spoon

3 Eggs should be medium unless otherwise stated.

4 Milk should be full fat unless otherwise stated.

5 Fresh herbs should be used unless otherwise stated. If unavailable use dried herbs as an alternative but halve the quantities stated.

6 Pepper should be freshly ground black pepper unless otherwise stated.

7 Ovens should be preheated to the specified temperature – if using a fan-assisted oven, follow the manufacturer's instructions for adjusting the time and temperature.

8 Measurements for canned food have been given as a standard metric equivalent.

Contents

Introduction

Chicken is now more popular than ever. It is healthy, nutritious, low in fat and easy to prepare and cook. Incredibly versatile, chicken can be cooked in so many ways as this book shows. With its mild flavour and tender, succulent flesh, it is the ideal choice for family meals and entertaining.

Types of Chicken

A wide range of poultry is now available and most birds are mass-produced but free-range chickens have the best flavour and it is well worth paying a little extra for them. In addition to barn-reared, traditional free range and organic free range chickens, you can also buy corn-fed chickens which have a distinctive yellow flesh and are fed a diet of maize for improved flavour and poussins which are tender, young chickens of 4–6 weeks, usually weighing 375-750 g (12 oz–1½ lb).

Buying, Storing and Preparing Chicken

When buying chicken, make sure that the wrapping is intact and not broken. Keep it as cool as possible until you get it home and then refrigerate or freeze immediately. Here are some safety guidelines to help you:

- If a fresh bird contains giblets, unwrap it, remove the giblets and store separately. Don't leave them inside the cavity of the chicken.
- Always cover a fresh bird and store on a separate shelf of the refrigerator to cooked foods.
- Always cook the chicken before the 'use by' date specified on the wrapping.
- The refrigerator temperature for storing chicken should be in the range 0–4°C.
- When freezing chicken, leave it in the original wrapping. Defrost thoroughly before cooking, especially whole chickens. It will take about 10 hours for a 1.5 kg (3 lb) chicken to defrost in a cool room (or three times as long in the refrigerator).
- Never freeze chicken which has already been frozen.
- Before and after handling raw chicken, wash your hands thoroughly. Use a clean chopping board and clean sharp knives and don't allow them to come into contact with any cooked food.

How to Tell if a Chicken is Cooked

Never eat under-cooked chicken – it must always be cooked right through. You can easily test whether a whole bird is cooked by inserting a skewer into the thickest part of the leg near where it joins the body. If the juices run clear then the chicken is cooked. You can perform the same test with chicken portions.

Stuffing Chicken

Never stuff the cavity of a bird; stuff the neck end only. If bacteria are present in the bird's juices, these could drip into the stuffing, and the stuffing may prevent the centre of the bird from being thoroughly cooked.

Making Chicken Stock

Home-made chicken stock has far more flavour than stock made with a cube or bouillon powder. Just put the chicken carcass (bones and skin) in a pan with 1 quartered onion, 1 thickly sliced carrot, 1 celery stick and 1 sliced leek. Add 1 bouquet garni and a few black peppercorns and cover with cold water. Bring to the boil, then skim off any scum that rises to the surface. Cover the pan, reduce the heat and simmer gently for about 2 hours. Strain the stock and set aside to cool. When it is cold, remove any fat from the surface and store, covered, in the refrigerator for a maximum of two days or freeze until required.

Jointing a Chicken

Use a sharp knife and poultry shears to make jointing easier.

1 Cut between the body and the leg joint on one side of the chicken. Twist outwards and then cut the leg away from the body. Repeat with the other leg.
2 Cut closely along both sides of the breastbone, removing as much flesh as possible.
3 Turn the bird over and cut along each side of the backbone to divide the chicken in half.
4 Cut off the wings, including some of the breast. You should end up with 6 chicken joints.

Soups and Starters

Chicken Broth

1 x 1.5 kg (3 lb) chicken
2 onions, chopped
2 garlic cloves, crushed
2 carrots, chopped
2 leeks, sliced
1 tablespoon dried tarragon
3 celery sticks, chopped
salt and pepper

Put the chicken into a large saucepan and cover with water. Bring to the boil and skim. Season with salt and pepper, then cover and simmer for 1½ hours.

Add the remaining ingredients and bring back to the boil. Simmer for a further 45 minutes.

Remove the chicken from the pan and cut off the breasts. Skin and dice the meat finely and return to the broth. Adjust the seasoning, if necessary, and serve. Save the rest of the chicken for another dish, such as a salad.

Serves 4–6

Variations:
Chicken Broth with Vermicelli
Add 125 g (4 oz) vermicelli, broken into very small pieces, to the broth with the diced chicken meat and simmer for a further 5 minutes.
Chicken Broth with Barley
Thirty minutes before the broth has finished simmering, add 75 g (3 oz) pearl barley.

Cock-a-Leekie Soup

In Scotland, this soup is traditionally served on Burns' Night. Today it makes use of the readily available supermarket chicken, but originally an old cock rooster would have been used!

1 x 1.25–1.5 kg (2½–3 lb) chicken, trussed, with the giblets (except liver and gall bladder)
1 bouquet garni
6 leeks, sliced lengthways
4–6 prunes, soaked overnight, halved and pitted
salt and pepper

Put the chicken and bouquet garni in a large saucepan, season well with salt and pepper and cover with water. Bring to the boil, then lower the heat, half cover and simmer very gently for 2 hours, skimming with a slotted spoon from time to time, if necessary, to remove any surface scum.

Add the leeks and more water to cover the bird if required, and continue to simmer, uncovered, for a further 1 hour or until the chicken is cooked and tender. Add the prunes 30 minutes before the end of the cooking time.

To serve, remove the chicken and discard the giblets and bouquet garni. Skim the broth and adjust the seasoning if necessary. The chicken can be carved and some of the meat returned to the soup and reheated before serving, or it may be eaten separately as a main course.

Serves 6

right: chicken broth, cock-a-leekie soup

Chicken and Rice Broth

This is a fine soup for using up the carcass of a roasted chicken.

1 chicken carcass and leftover chicken, diced
½ teaspoon salt
6 black peppercorns, finely crushed
1 bay leaf
1 bouquet garni
2 carrots, sliced
3 celery sticks, chopped
50 g (2 oz) long-grain rice
To garnish:
chopped parsley
50 g (2 oz) blanched almonds, chopped

Put the chicken carcass and any meat into a large saucepan, cover with water and add the remaining ingredients. Bring to the boil. Lower the heat, cover the pan and simmer gently for 2 hours, skimming with a slotted spoon to remove any scum. Add more water if the liquid in the pan becomes low.

Discard the carcass, making sure every scrap of meat is left in the broth. Skim off any fat, using a spoon or kitchen paper. Discard the bay leaf and bouquet garni and adjust the seasoning to taste.

Serve the broth piping hot, scattered with plenty of parsley and the chopped almonds.

Serves 4

Sweetcorn and Chicken Soup

For this soup use a carcass that still has a certain amount of meat left on the bones. If you don't have a chicken carcass, use 1 chicken portion and 2–3 stock cubes. If a chunky soup is preferred, there is no need to purée it – simply add the green or red pepper and chicken and serve.

1 chicken carcass, raw or cooked
1.2 litres (2 pints) water
1 bouquet garni
50 g (2 oz) butter or margarine
1 small onion, finely chopped
40 g (1½ oz) plain flour
½ teaspoon curry powder (optional)
1 teaspoon tomato purée
1 x 325 g (11 oz) can sweetcorn kernels, drained
3 tomatoes, skinned and chopped
dash of Worcestershire sauce
pinch of garlic powder
salt and pepper
1 small green or red pepper, cored and deseeded, to garnish

Put the chicken carcass into a saucepan with the water, bouquet garni and salt and pepper to taste. Bring to the boil, skim well, then cover and simmer gently for about 1 hour. Stir once or twice while the stock is cooking.

Strain off the stock from the bones and reserve 1 litre (1¾ pints). Pick about 50 g (2 oz) of the meat from the carcass and chop finely.

Melt the butter or margarine in a large saucepan and fry the onion until soft. Stir in the flour, curry powder, if using, and tomato purée, and cook for 1 minute. Gradually add the reserved stock and bring to the boil. Add the sweetcorn kernels, tomatoes, Worcestershire sauce and garlic powder. Cover the pan and simmer for 20 minutes.

Meanwhile, cut a quarter of the pepper into thin strips and finely chop the remainder. Bring a small pan of water to the boil, add both and cook for 5 minutes, then drain.

If a smooth soup is preferred, cool the soup slightly, then either press through a sieve or purée in a blender or food processor and return to a clean pan with the chopped pepper and reserved chicken meat. Season to taste and simmer for 2–3 minutes.

Serve the soup hot, garnished with the strips of pepper.

Serves 4

right: chicken velouté soup

Chicken Velouté Soup

1 x 1.5 kg (3 lb) chicken

2 onions, quartered

2 garlic cloves, crushed

2 carrots, sliced

2 leeks, sliced

2 celery sticks, chopped

1 tablespoon chopped tarragon

75 g (3 oz) butter

50 g (2 oz) plain flour

2 egg yolks

125 ml (4 fl oz) double cream

salt and pepper

1 tablespoon chopped parsley,
  to garnish

Put the chicken into a large saucepan and cover with water. Add the onions, garlic, carrots, leeks and celery. Bring to the boil and skim. Add the tarragon, then cover and simmer for 1½ hours, or until the chicken is cooked.

Remove the chicken from the pan and cut off the breasts. Skin and dice the meat finely. Save the remainder of the chicken for another dish. Strain the broth and reserve 1.8 litres (3 pints).

Melt the butter in a clean saucepan and stir in the flour. Cook until the roux (butter and flour mixture) is a very pale straw colour. Stir in the reserved strained broth. Simmer gently until smooth and thickened, and then add salt and pepper to taste.

Beat together the egg yolks and cream. Remove the pan from the heat and beat in the egg yolk mixture. Return to the heat and heat through gently. Stir in the diced chicken breast and serve sprinkled with the parsley.

Serves 6

Variation:
Cream of Chicken Soup

Do not allow the butter and flour roux to colour (cook for only 1 minute). Omit the egg yolks and stir in the cream just before serving.

Spiced Chicken Soup

Macadamias are usually sold shelled and the kernels easily break into fragments.

1.5 litres (2½ pints) water
1 x 1.25 kg (2½ lb) chicken, quartered
4 raw king prawns (with shells on)
2 macadamia nuts, chopped
4 shallots, chopped
2 garlic cloves, crushed
2 teaspoons grated fresh root ginger
pinch of turmeric
pinch of chilli powder
4 tablespoons vegetable oil
1 tablespoon light soy sauce
75 g (3 oz) bean sprouts
1 potato, cut into very thin rounds
salt and pepper

Put the water in a pan and bring to the boil. Add the chicken, prawns and a little salt and pepper. Cover the pan and simmer for 40 minutes. Strain and reserve 1.2 litres (2 pints) of the liquid. Shred the meat from the chicken and shell and chop the prawns. Set aside.

Purée the macadamias, shallots, garlic and ginger in a blender or food processor. Add the turmeric and chilli powder and mix well.

Heat 2 tablespoons of the oil in a wok or frying pan, add the spice paste and fry for a few seconds. Stir in 300 ml (½ pint) of the reserved liquid together with the soy sauce, chicken and prawns. Simmer for 10 minutes. Add the remaining

Chicken Mulligatawny

50 g (2 oz) plain flour
1 tablespoon curry powder
40 g (1½ oz) margarine
1 onion, chopped
4 streaky bacon rashers, rind removed
   and minced
250 g (8 oz) chicken portions
1.8 litres (3 pints) water
1 teaspoon salt
juice of ½ lemon
1 teaspoon brown sugar
lemon slices, to garnish

Sift the flour and curry powder together. Melt the margarine in a saucepan and add the curry powder mixture. Cook, stirring, for 2 minutes. Add the onion, bacon and chicken and brown lightly. Add the water, bring to the boil and skim. Add the salt, lemon juice and sugar, then cover the pan and simmer gently for 1 hour.

Remove the chicken, and skin and chop the meat finely. Return to the pan and reheat. Adjust the seasoning, if necessary. Serve at once, garnished with a lemon slice.

Serves 6

cooking liquid and simmer for 10 minutes. Add the bean sprouts and cook for a further 3 minutes.

Meanwhile, fry the potato slices in the remaining oil until crisp. Serve the soup hot, garnished with the fried potato.

Serves 4–6

left: chicken mulligatawny
below: chicken and mushroom soup

Chicken and Mushroom Soup

250 g (8 oz) chicken portions
1 onion, chopped
1 garlic clove, crushed
1 teaspoon Worcestershire sauce
250 g (8 oz) mushrooms, sliced
1 bay leaf
2 teaspoons arrowroot
1 tablespoon water
125 ml (4 fl oz) double cream
salt and pepper

Put the chicken in a saucepan with the onion, garlic, Worcestershire sauce, mushrooms, bay leaf and enough water to cover. Bring to the boil and skim the surface. Cover the pan and simmer gently for 1 hour.

Remove the chicken and bay leaf. Skin and finely chop the meat. Season the broth with salt and pepper to taste. Dissolve the arrowroot in 1 tablespoon water, stirring well, and add to the broth. Stir well and simmer for 5 minutes. Stir in the cream and chopped chicken meat and heat through gently. Serve immediately.

Serves 4–6

Chicken Liver Dip

50 g (2 oz) butter
1 onion, finely chopped
1 garlic clove, crushed
250 g (8 oz) chicken livers
1 bay leaf
1 tablespoon brandy or port
3–4 tablespoons natural yogurt
1 teaspoon capers, finely chopped
    (optional)
salt and pepper
parsley sprigs, to garnish

Melt the butter in a frying pan. Add the onion and garlic and fry gently until soft but not coloured, for about 3 minutes.

Wash and drain the chicken livers thoroughly. Chop them roughly, then add to the pan with the bay leaf and cook gently for about 10 minutes, stirring frequently, until tender. Cool slightly and discard the bay leaf.

Purée the liver, onion and garlic in a blender or food processor, adding the brandy or port, and then spoon into a serving bowl.

Beat in sufficient yogurt to give a creamy consistency. Season to taste with salt and pepper and mix in the capers, if using.

Leave to cool. When cold, add extra yogurt if necessary, then cover and chill in the refrigerator until ready for use.

Garnish with parsley and serve with a selection of cocktail biscuits, crisps, carrot and celery sticks, cauliflower florets and chunks of cucumber. If preferred, serve the dip in individual pots.

Serves 8

Chicken Mousse

70 g (2½ oz) packet aspic jelly powder
600 ml (1 pint) chicken stock
500 g (1 lb) cooked chicken meat, shredded
100 ml (3½ fl oz) dry sherry
1 teaspoon dried tarragon
freshly ground white pepper
300 ml (½ pint) double cream
2 teaspoons tomato purée
watercress sprigs, to garnish

Dampen a 1.5 litre (2½ pint) mould. Make up the aspic with the stock, according to the instructions on the packet. Allow to cool until on the point of setting.

Put the aspic, chicken, sherry, tarragon and a little pepper into a blender or food processor and blend until smooth. Beat in the cream and tomato purée.

Turn into the mould. Chill in the refrigerator until set. Turn out to serve, garnished with watercress.

Serves 8

Layered Turkey Mousse

400 ml (14 fl oz) liquid aspic
2 tablespoons dry vermouth or sherry
250 g (8 oz) cooked white turkey
    meat, chopped
50 g (2 oz) butter
50 g (2 oz) plain flour
600 ml (1 pint) milk
1 egg, separated
pinch of mustard powder
2 teaspoons creamed horseradish
25 g (1 oz) powdered gelatine
4 tablespoons hot water
75 g (3 oz) cooked ham, minced
75 g (3 oz) cooked tongue, minced
1 tablespoon chopped capers
1 tablespoon lemon juice
2 tablespoons mayonnaise
375 g (12 oz) cooked dark turkey
    meat, chopped
salt and pepper
To garnish:
cucumber slices
cream cheese or thick mayonnaise
tomato or radish roses (see
    Cook's Tips)

Grease a 1.2 litre (2 pint) loaf tin. Mix the hot aspic with the vermouth or sherry, and cool. Pour a 5 mm (¼ inch) layer of the aspic into the loaf tin and chill until set.

Mix the remaining aspic with the white turkey meat and spoon into the tin. Chill in the refrigerator until set.

Melt the butter in a pan. Add the flour and cook for 1 minute.

Gradually add the milk, bring to the boil and cook for 2 minutes, stirring constantly. Season with salt and pepper to taste. Pour half the sauce into a bowl, cover and leave to cool. Stir the egg yolk, mustard and horseradish into the remaining sauce and leave to cool.

Dissolve half the gelatine in about 2 tablespoons hot water and stir into the horseradish sauce with the ham and tongue. Allow to cool. Whisk the egg white until it forms stiff peaks and fold into the cooled sauce with a metal spoon. Spoon into the tin and chill until set.

Add the capers, lemon juice and mayonnaise to the remaining sauce. Dissolve the remaining gelatine in about 2 tablespoons hot water and stir into the sauce with the dark turkey meat. Spoon over the set ham layer in the tin and chill until set.

To serve, dip the tin briefly into hot water, then invert on to a serving plate. Garnish with cucumber slices, piped cream cheese or mayonnaise and tomato or radish roses.

Serves 8–10

Cook's Tips: To make a tomato rose, start at the smooth end and carefully cut away the tomato skin in one continuous strip. Roll up to form a rose and secure with half a cocktail stick. To make a radish rose, cut a narrow slice from the root end of the radish. Cut several rows of 'petals', keeping each petal joined by its base to the radish. Stagger the rows so that the petals alternate with those in the previous row. Leave the radish in iced water for several hours to open out.

above: layered turkey mousse

Smoked Chicken Pâté

The pâté can be made up to 3 days in advance, if kept covered and chilled.

250 g (8 oz) smoked chicken, skinned and chopped

rind of ½ lemon
3 tablespoons lemon juice
1 tablespoon snipped chives
150 ml (¼ pint) soured cream
50 g (2 oz) butter
salt and pepper

To garnish:
lemon quarters or twists
chive bundles

Place all the ingredients in a blender or food processor. Purée until smooth and creamy.

Spoon into 1 large or 6 small serving dishes, cover with cling film and chill in the refrigerator until set.

Serve with crackers, garnished with lemon quarters or twists and chive bundles.

Serves 6

Pâté de Campagne

oil, for brushing
8 streaky bacon rashers, rinds removed
500 g (1 lb) pig's liver
500 g (1 lb) chicken livers
250 g (8 oz) pork back fat or fatty belly pork
175 g (6 oz) fresh white breadcrumbs
2 eggs, beaten
2 garlic cloves, crushed with ½ teaspoon salt
75 ml (3 fl oz) red wine
2 tablespoons brandy (optional)
2 teaspoons chopped thyme or 1 teaspoon dried thyme
40–50 g (1½–2 oz) shelled pistachio nuts, coarsely chopped
pepper

Brush the inside of a 1 kg (2 lb) loaf tin or a 1.2 litre (2 pint) earthenware dish with oil. Stretch the bacon rashers with the blade of

a knife, then use to evenly line the base and sides of the tin or dish. Set aside.

Mince together the pig's liver, chicken livers and pork, then place in a bowl. Add the remaining ingredients with pepper to taste, and stir well.

Spoon into the tin or dish and level the surface. Cover with foil, then stand the tin in a roasting tin half-filled with hot water. Bake in a preheated oven, 160°C (325°F), Gas Mark 3, for 2½ hours, until the pâté and the juices are faintly pink.

Remove from the oven and pour off the excess fat from the tin or dish. Leave until cool and then place heavy weights on top of the foil to press the pâté into a firm shape for slicing. Set aside until completely cold, then place in the refrigerator and chill overnight.

Run a knife around the edge of the pâté to release the bacon from the tin and then turn the pâté out on to a serving board. Serve cut into thick slices.

Serves 8–10

left: smoked chicken pâté
right: pâté de campagne

Duck Liver Pâté

150 g (5 oz) unsalted butter
1 duck liver
2 shallots, chopped
1 x 1.5 kg (3 lb) cold roast duck, skinned and boned
grated rind and juice of 1 orange
4 tablespoons port
pinch of powdered bay
pinch of dried rosemary
salt and pepper

Melt 15 g (½ oz) of the butter in a saucepan. Add the liver and fry quickly until lightly browned on both sides. Remove from the pan and allow to cool.

Melt a further 15 g (½ oz) butter in the pan. Add the shallots and fry gently until soft but not brown.

Pass the liver, shallots, duck meat and 75 g (3 oz) of the remaining butter through the fine blade of a mincer twice. Mix together well. Alternatively, chop coarsely in a blender or food processor.

Stir in the orange rind and juice, port, herbs, and salt and pepper to taste. Spoon into a terrine and seal with the remaining butter, melted and clarified (see page 19). Leave in the refrigerator overnight to set before serving.

Serves 6

Brandied Duck Pâté

250 g (8 oz) streaky bacon rashers,
  rinded
250 g (8 oz) belly of pork, skinned,
  boned and minced
1 x 1.75 kg (3½ lb) oven-ready duck
  (excluding giblets), skinned, boned
  and minced
250 g (8 oz) lean pork (e.g. fillet or
  leg), minced
250 g (8 oz) chicken livers, minced
1 egg, beaten

1 garlic clove, crushed
2 tablespoons brandy
¼ teaspoon ground allspice
grated rind of 1 orange
2 tablespoons chopped parsley
salt and pepper

Stretch the bacon rashers with the
back of a knife and arrange
crossways to line the base and sides
of a 1 kg (2 lb) loaf tin.

Mix the belly of pork with the
duck, lean pork, chicken livers,
beaten egg, garlic, brandy, allspice,
orange rind, parsley and salt and
pepper. Spoon into the prepared tin

and level the surface. Cover with a
piece of buttered foil.

Place in a roasting tin half-full of
water. Cook in a preheated oven,
180°C (350°F), Gas Mark 4, for
2¼ hours.

Allow to cool slightly. Cover with
a double thickness of foil, place a
weight on top and leave to go cold.
Chill the pâté thoroughly, still
weighted down, for at least
24 hours, before turning out to
serve. Cut into slices and serve with
a green salad and toast.

Serves 8

Chicken Liver Pâté

250 g (8 oz) chicken livers, trimmed
1 onion, chopped
1 garlic clove, peeled
50 g (2 oz) wholemeal bread
3 tablespoons skimmed milk
1 egg
50 g (2 oz) margarine
2 teaspoons chopped mixed herbs
2 tablespoons Greek yogurt
salt and pepper
To garnish:
lemon wedges
parsley sprigs

Place all the ingredients in a blender or food processor and blend until smooth. Divide equally between 4 small ovenproof dishes or ramekins. Cover with greased foil.

Place in a roasting tin with sufficient hot water to come halfway up the sides of the dishes. Cook in a preheated oven, 180°C (350°F), Gas Mark 4, for about 40 minutes, until just set. Remove from the tin and leave until cool before chilling in the refrigerator.

Serve lightly chilled with toast or salad, garnished with lemon wedges and parsley sprigs.

Serves 4

left: brandied duck pâté

Chicken Liver, Port and Pistachio Terrine

140 g (4½ oz) unsalted butter
375 g (12 oz) chicken livers, trimmed
1 teaspoon juniper berries, crushed
1 mace blade, crumbled
¼ teaspoon ground allspice
1 garlic clove, crushed
4 tablespoons port
50 g (2 oz) shelled pistachio nuts, halved
175 g (6 oz) unsalted butter, clarified (see Cook's Tip)
salt and pepper

Melt 50 g (2 oz) of the butter in a large frying pan. When it is beginning to bubble, add the chicken livers. Cook, stirring constantly, for 4–5 minutes, until they are firm but still pink inside. Remove the livers from the pan.

Add the berries, mace, allspice, garlic and port to the pan. Allow to bubble for 1 minute, then pour the mixture over the chicken livers, scraping up any sediment from the bottom of the pan with a spatula.

Purée the chicken livers in a blender or food processor, or mash with a fork and push through a coarse sieve. Season generously with salt and pepper.

Melt the rest of the butter and beat into the chicken liver purée, then put half the mixture into a serving bowl.

Reserve about 15 of the pistachio nuts, then scatter the rest over the chicken liver pâté in the serving bowl. Cover with the remaining pâté, then push the reserved nuts into the top of the pâté at an angle, leaving just the tips exposed.

To finish, pour the clarified butter over the pâté. Chill for at least 3 hours before serving.

Serves 8

Cook's Tip: To clarify butter, melt unsalted butter in a pan until it is just beginning to bubble. Remove from the heat and strain into a bowl, preferably through muslin, leaving the white sediment behind.

Duck, Orange and Brandy Terrine

1 large duck portion or 250 g (8 oz) duck flesh, including some skin and fat
125 g (4 oz) lean bacon rashers, rind removed
1 onion
grated rind of ½ orange
2 tablespoons orange juice
1 tablespoon brandy
1 egg, beaten
1 small garlic clove, crushed
salt and pepper
To garnish:
orange slices
a little liquid aspic jelly (optional)
bay leaves

Strip the flesh off the duck portion and then mince finely with the bacon and onion in a mincer, blender or food processor.

Transfer to a bowl and beat in the orange rind and juice, brandy, egg, salt, plenty of pepper and the garlic until the mixture is evenly blended and quite smooth.

Grease a 600 ml (1 pint) casserole or terrine dish and spoon in the mixture, pressing down well.

Cover lightly with foil or a lid and stand in a roasting tin containing 4 cm (1½ inches) water.

Cook in a preheated oven, 180°C (350°F), Gas Mark 4, for 30 minutes. Uncover and continue cooking for a further 35–40 minutes, until the terrine is cooked through. Remove from the roasting tin and set aside until completely cold.

Garnish with slices of orange and pour over a layer of aspic jelly, if using, which is on the point of setting. Chill in the refrigerator until set.

Before serving, add bay leaves to complete the garnish. Serve with crusty bread or hot toast and butter.

Serves 4–6

Individual Turkey Liver Terrines

500 g (1 lb) turkey livers
250 g (8 oz) boneless belly of pork, skin removed
175 g (6 oz) streaky bacon, rind removed
1 onion
2 garlic cloves, crushed
2 tablespoons sherry
dash of Worcestershire sauce
1 egg, beaten
salt and pepper
To garnish:
cucumber slices
stuffed olives, sliced
200 ml (7 fl oz) liquid aspic (optional)

Grease 8 ovenproof ramekins. Blanch half the turkey livers in boiling water for 2 minutes. Drain well. Finely mince the raw and blanched turkey livers with the pork, bacon and onion. Add the garlic, sherry, Worcestershire sauce, beaten egg, and salt and pepper to taste. Spoon into the ramekins and level the surfaces. Cover each with buttered foil.

Place in a roasting pan half-full of water. Cook in a preheated oven, 180°C (350°F), Gas Mark 4, for about 1 hour, or until the juices run clear when the terrines are pierced.

Allow to cool slightly. Cover with a double thickness of foil, place a weight on top of each terrine and leave to cool for about 4 hours.

Garnish with slices of cucumber and stuffed olives. Spoon over the liquid aspic, if using, and chill to set. Serve lightly chilled, with toast.

Serves 8

right: individual turkey liver terrines

Whisky Terrine

The terrine can be made up to 4 days in advance, if kept covered and chilled in the refrigerator.

125 g (4 oz) butter
1 large onion, chopped
1 garlic clove, crushed
125 g (4 oz) streaky bacon, rind removed and chopped
250 g (8 oz) chicken livers
125 g (4 oz) button mushrooms
150 ml (¼ pint) whisky
finely grated rind of 1 lemon
2 tablespoons lemon juice
1½ tablespoons chopped parsley
2½ tablespoons fresh breadcrumbs
2 small bay leaves
3 allspice berries
salt and pepper

Melt the butter in a large pan. Add the onion and garlic and cook over a gentle heat for 10 minutes. Add the bacon, livers and mushrooms and cook for a further 5 minutes.

Add the whisky, lemon rind and juice and salt and pepper. Cover and simmer for 10–15 minutes.

Purée in a blender or food processor until smooth. Add the parsley and breadcrumbs and blend again to mix.

Spoon into a serving dish and level the surface. Press the bay leaves and allspice berries into the top. Cover with cling film and chill in the refrigerator to set.

Serves 6

Smoked Chicken with Mango

2 ripe mangoes, peeled, pitted and cut into thin strips
3 tablespoons olive oil
1 tablespoon wine vinegar
2 teaspoons snipped chives
¼ teaspoon cayenne pepper
250 g (8 oz) smoked chicken, skinned and thinly sliced
2 hard-boiled eggs, shelled and sliced
salt
snipped chives, to garnish

Place the mango strips in a shallow dish. Beat the oil with the wine vinegar, chives, cayenne pepper and salt. Pour over the mango and toss to coat. Cover and leave to marinate for at least 1 hour.

Arrange the chicken slices with the hard-boiled eggs on 4 individual serving dishes.

Remove the mango from the dressing with a slotted spoon and arrange attractively over the chicken and egg mixture. Spoon over the remaining dressing and garnish with chives.

Serves 4

Cook's Tip: To peel a mango, spear one end with a fork. Using a sharp knife, slit along the fruit's skin lengthways to divide it into 4 sections. Grip each section of skin between your thumb and the knife and gently pull away to strip it off. To release the flesh, cut into the stone, holding the knife along the length of the fruit. Cut the flesh away cleanly in segments.

above: smoked chicken with mango
right: parmesan chicken wings

Parmesan Chicken Wings

250 g (8 oz) dried breadcrumbs

125 g (4 oz) Parmesan cheese, freshly
  grated

1 teaspoon dried basil

1 teaspoon dried thyme

1 teaspoon salt

12 chicken wings, cut in half and tips
  cut off

175 g (6 oz) butter or margarine,
  melted

To serve (optional):

lettuce leaves

2 lemons, sliced

Mix together the breadcrumbs,
cheese, herbs and salt, and spread
out on a flat plate.

Dip the wings in the melted
butter, then roll in the seasoned
crumb mixture. Lay the wings in a
single layer on 1 or 2 large baking
sheets, well spaced out.

Place the baking sheets in a
preheated oven, 200°C (400°F),
Gas Mark 6 and bake for about
45 minutes, until crisp and golden
brown. If using 2 baking sheets, put
them on separate shelves and
reverse their oven position halfway
through the baking time. Serve on
lettuce leaves, with lemon slices,
if liked.

Serves 8

Shredded Chicken

Boning and skinning a whole chicken takes time and patience, but it is often a cheaper alternative to buying portions.

2 green chillies, deseeded and
  coarsely chopped
3 garlic cloves, peeled
50 g (2 oz) fresh root ginger, peeled
1 large Spanish onion, coarsely
  chopped
1 tablespoon vinegar
1 x 1.5 kg (3 lb) chicken or 4 chicken
  breasts, skinned, boned and
  shredded
3 teaspoons ground cumin
2 teaspoons freshly ground black
  pepper
40 g (1½ oz) ghee or 3 tablespoons
  vegetable oil
2 green peppers, cored, deseeded
  and sliced
juice of 1 lemon

Grind the green chillies, garlic, ginger, onion and vinegar to a paste using a pestle and mortar. Alternatively, blend to a paste using a blender or food processor. Place the shredded chicken and the paste in a large bowl or dish, mix thoroughly, then cover and set aside for 1 hour to marinate.

Add the cumin and black pepper to the marinated mixture and mix well. Heat the ghee or vegetable oil in a large pan, add the chicken, then cover and fry over a low heat for 15–20 minutes.

Uncover the pan and add the sliced green peppers. Fry for a further 10 minutes, until the mixture is fairly dry and the chicken is cooked. Sprinkle with the lemon juice just before serving.

Serve as a side dish with a main course curry or simply with bread for a lighter meal.

Serves 4

Indian Chicken Kebabs

4 boneless, skinless chicken breasts
250 g (8 oz) cauliflower florets
2 onions, cut into thin wedges
lemon quarters, to garnish
Marinade:
1 onion, grated
2 garlic cloves, crushed
2.5 cm (1 inch) piece of fresh root
  ginger , peeled and grated
pinch of cayenne pepper
3 tablespoons lemon juice
1 tablespoon ground coriander

1 teaspoon ground cumin
1 teaspoon garam masala
1 teaspoon ground cardamom
½ teaspoon ground cinnamon
1 teaspoon red or orange food
  colouring (optional)
150 ml (¼ pint) natural yogurt

Cut the chicken into bite-sized pieces and place in a bowl.

To make the marinade, mix all the ingredients together in a bowl and pour over the chicken pieces. Toss well to coat. Cover and leave in a cool place to marinate for about 4 hours.

Cook the cauliflower florets in salted boiling water for 3–4 minutes. Drain thoroughly.

Remove the chicken from the marinade with a slotted spoon, reserving the marinade. Thread on to 4 skewers, alternating with the onion wedges and cauliflower .

Brush the kebabs with the marinade and cook under a preheated hot grill, for about 10–12 minutes, turning frequently and brushing occasionally with the remaining marinade.

Garnish with lemon wedges and serve with rice and mango chutney.

Serves 4

Chicken Tikka

750 g (1½ lb) boneless, skinless
  chicken breasts, cubed
Marinade:
150 ml (¼ pint) natural yogurt
1 tablespoon grated fresh root ginger
2 garlic cloves, crushed
1 teaspoon chilli powder
1 tablespoon ground coriander
½ teaspoon salt
juice of 1 lemon

2 tablespoons vegetable oil
To garnish:
1 onion, sliced
2 tomatoes, quartered
4 lemon wedges
parsley sprigs

To make the marinade, mix all the ingredients together in a bowl. Add the chicken cubes, stir well to coat, then cover and leave in the refrigerator overnight.

Thread the chicken on to 4 skewers and cook under a preheated hot grill for 5–6 minutes, turning frequently.

Remove the chicken from the skewers and arrange on warmed individual serving plates. Serve garnished with onion slices, tomato quarters, lemon wedges and parsley sprigs.

Serves 4

Devilled Chicken Livers

500 g (1 lb) chicken livers
50 g (2 oz) butter
2 tablespoons Worcestershire sauce
6 tablespoons red wine or chicken
  stock
4 teaspoons Dijon mustard
dash of Tabasco sauce
salt and pepper
toast triangles, to serve
To garnish:
small tomato wedges
parsley sprigs

Prepare the chicken livers by removing any dark or yellowish bits. Chop the livers roughly.

Heat the butter in a large frying pan and cook the livers briskly until browned on all sides. Add the Worcestershire sauce, wine or stock, mustard, Tabasco sauce, and salt and pepper to taste. Stir to blend. Continue cooking until the livers are tender but still slightly pink in the centre.

Spoon the livers on to toast triangles and garnish with small tomato wedges and parsley sprigs. Serve hot.

Serves 8

left: chicken tikka

Chicken and Mushroom Vol-au-Vents

250 g (8 oz) puff pastry, defrosted, if
  frozen
beaten egg, to glaze
Filling:
50 g (2 oz) butter
25 g (1 oz) plain flour
300 ml (½ pint) milk
125g (4 oz) mushrooms, sliced
175 g (6 oz) cooked chicken meat,
  chopped finely
salt and pepper

Dampen a baking sheet. Roll out the pastry to a 5 mm (¼ inch) thickness on a floured board. Cut the pastry into 4 rounds, using a 9 cm (3½ inch) pastry cutter and place on the dampened baking sheet. Cut halfway through the centre of each round with a 5 cm (2 inch) pastry cutter.

To make the filling, melt 25 g (1 oz) of the butter in a heavy-based saucepan. Remove from the heat and mix in the flour, then gradually stir in the milk until smooth. Return to the heat and bring the white sauce to the boil, stirring constantly until thickened.

Melt the remaining butter in another saucepan, add the mushrooms and cook for 3 minutes. Stir in the chicken, prepared white sauce and salt and pepper to taste. Leave the filling to cook very gently while baking the vol-au-vent cases.

Brush the pastries with beaten egg and bake in a preheated oven, 220°C (425°F), Gas Mark 7, for 20 minutes, until well risen and crisp. Allow to cool slightly, then, with a sharp knife, carefully remove the pastry lids. Scoop out any soft pastry from the centre of the cases.

Divide the filling among the pastry cases, replace the lids and serve at once.

Serves 4

Variations:
If preferred, use 75 g (3 oz) finely chopped cooked ham in place of the mushrooms; add with the chicken. Instead of 4 rounds, cut 8 x 5 cm (2 inch) vol-au-vents, then stamp 2.5 cm (1 inch) circles halfway through.

Savoury Chicken Horns

250 g (8 oz) puff pastry, defrosted, if
  frozen
beaten egg, to glaze
Filling:
40 g (1½ oz) butter or margarine
1 large celery stick, finely chopped
25 g (1 oz) plain flour
200 ml (7 fl oz) milk or chicken stock
2 tablespoons thick mayonnaise
1½–2 teaspoons tarragon mustard or
  French mustard and ½ teaspoon
  dried tarragon
1 red pimento, chopped
250 g (8 oz) seedless green grapes
125 g (4 oz) cooked chicken meat,
  finely chopped
salt and pepper
parsley sprigs, to garnish

Roll out the pastry thinly on a
floured surface to about 30 x 11 cm
(12 x 4 ½ inches) and cut into strips
about 2.5 cm (1 inch) wide.

Lightly grease 4 large or 8 small
metal cream horn tins. Grease a
baking sheet. Brush the strips of
pastry with beaten egg and wind
round the horn tins, keeping the
glazed side outwards and just
overlapping as you wind.

Place the horns on the baking
sheet and cook in a preheated oven,
220°C (425°F), Gas Mark 7, for
15–20 minutes, until golden brown.

Remove the tins from the pastry horns and cool on a wire rack.

Meanwhile, melt the butter or margarine in a saucepan and fry the celery gently for 2–3 minutes. Stir in the flour and cook for 1 minute, then gradually add the milk or stock, still stirring, and boil for 2 minutes.

Stir in the mayonnaise, mustard and pimento. Season with salt and pepper, then allow to cool. Peel and halve 75 g (3 oz) of the grapes and stir into the mustard and pimento sauce with the chicken.

Spoon the filling into the horns and garnish with the remaining grapes and parsley sprigs.

Serves 4

Chicken Tartlets

Lemon pastry:

175 g (6 oz) plain flour

salt

75 g (3 oz) butter, diced

grated rind of ½ lemon

2 tablespoons iced water

Filling:

275 g (9 oz) cooked chicken , finely
  chopped

50 g (2 oz) walnuts, coarsely
  chopped

125 g (4 oz) Gruyère cheese, grated

2 eggs, beaten

150 ml (¼ pint) milk

pinch of grated nutmeg

salt and pepper

watercress sprigs, to garnish

Grease 4 Yorkshire pudding tins or small quiche tins. To make the pastry, sift the flour and salt into a bowl. Rub in the butter with the fingertips until the mixture resembles fine breadcrumbs. Stir in the lemon rind and iced water, and bind to a firm but pliable dough.

Roll out the pastry on a lightly floured surface and cut out rounds large enough to line the tins. Prick the bases well with a fork and line each with greaseproof paper. Fill with baking beans, dried peas or lentils. Bake in a preheated oven, 200°C (400°F), Gas Mark 6, for 10 minutes. Remove the paper and baking beans, and reduce the oven temperature to 180°C (350°F), Gas Mark 4.

Put the chicken and walnuts in the tartlet cases and sprinkle with the grated cheese. Beat the eggs and milk together with the nutmeg and seasoning and pour over the chicken and cheese mixture.

Bake in the oven for about 15 minutes, until the custard sets and the tartlets are golden brown. Serve garnished with watercress.

Serves 4

Variations:

Ring the changes when using shortcrust pastry by adding flavours complementary to the fillings. To a basic 175 g (6 oz) recipe add one of the following: 25 g (1 oz) chopped nuts; grated rind of ½ small orange; 1–2 teaspoons curry powder or ground cinnamon; 1½–2 teaspoons dried herbs; 1–2 teaspoons turmeric; or ½ small onion, chopped and cooked.

Salads

Chicken and Sweetcorn Salad

250 g (8 oz) cooked chicken meat,
   shredded
1 tablespoon soy sauce
500 g (1 lb) can sweetcorn, drained
   and rinsed
salt and pepper
lettuce leaves, to serve

Put the chicken and soy sauce in a bowl, mix together, cover and leave to marinate for 30 minutes.

Mix the marinated chicken with the sweetcorn and season to taste with salt and pepper.

Line a salad bowl with the lettuce leaves and pile the chicken mixture in to the centre. Serve immediately.

Serves 4

Chicken and Pepper Salad

250 g (8 oz) cooked chicken meat,
   shredded
4 tablespoons Vinaigrette Dressing
   (see page 35)
1 large green or red pepper, cored,
   deseeded and thinly sliced
300 g (10 oz) cold cooked rice
salt and pepper

Put the chicken and vinaigrette dressing in a bowl, mix together, cover and leave in a cool place to marinate for 10 minutes.

Mix the marinated chicken with the green pepper and rice, and season with salt and pepper to taste. Cover loosely and leave in a cool place for 1 hour before serving.

Serves 4

left: chicken and sweetcorn salad
right: spiced chicken salad

Spiced Chicken Salad

175 g (6 oz) cooked chicken meat,
  shredded
1–2 tomatoes, skinned, deseeded and
  chopped (see Cook's Tip)
1 green chilli, deseeded and very
  finely chopped
½ cucumber, chopped
½ lettuce, coarsely shredded
1 small onion, finely sliced
1 green pepper, cored, deseeded and
  thinly sliced

1–2 coriander sprigs, chopped
2 teaspoons cumin seeds
juice of 1 lemon
salt and pepper

Mix together the chicken and all
the remaining ingredients in a large
serving bowl. Season to taste with
salt and pepper.

If possible, leave the mixture to
stand for 30 minutes so that the
flavours can develop before serving.
Serve as a side dish to a main meal
or as a starter.

Serves 3–4

Cook's Tip: To skin, deseed and chop
tomatoes, first cut out the cores of the
tomatoes using the point of a small
sharp knife. Lightly score a cross in the
other end of the tomatoes, then
immerse them in boiling water for 8–15
seconds, depending on their ripeness,
until the skin curls from the crosses. Lift
the tomatoes from the water, cool
slightly, then peel off the skin. Halve the
tomatoes crosswise and squeeze and
scrape out the seeds. Chop the flesh.

Chicken, Lettuce and Tomato Salad

3 tablespoons thick mayonnaise
250 g (8 oz) cooked chicken meat, shredded
4 ripe tomatoes, skinned and sliced
1 crisp lettuce, torn into small pieces

Mix the mayonnaise with the chicken. Arrange the tomatoes and lettuce on a serving platter and pile the chicken mixture on top.

Serves 4

Chicken, Orange and Rice Salad

250 g (8 oz) cooked chicken meat, shredded
300 g (10 oz) cold cooked rice
300 g (10 oz) can mandarin orange segments, drained
4 tablespoons olive oil
salt and pepper
chopped parsley, to garnish

Mix the chicken, rice and mandarin segments in a large bowl. Toss gently in the olive oil and season lightly with salt and pepper to taste. Sprinkle with parsley and serve.

Serves 4

Chicken, Noodle and Parmesan Salad

4 tablespoons olive oil
250 g (8 oz) cooked chicken meat, shredded
375 g (12 oz) cold cooked noodles
75 g (3 oz) Parmesan cheese, grated
salt and pepper
watercress sprigs, to garnish

Mix 1 tablespoon of the oil with the chicken and season with salt and pepper to taste. Toss the noodles in the remaining oil and mix together with the chicken. Spoon into a serving dish and sprinkle with the grated cheese. Garnish with watercress sprigs and serve.

Serves 4

above: chicken, lettuce and tomato salad; chicken noodle and parmesan salad; chicken, orange and rice salad

Turkey and Papaya Salad

Remember to wear rubber gloves when handling chillies or you risk transferring the painful oils to your eyes.

500 g (1 lb) cold cooked turkey, skinned
375 g (12 oz) green peppers, cored, deseeded and thinly sliced
1–2 fresh green chillies, deseeded and thinly sliced
1 large ripe papaya, peeled and deseeded
150 ml (¼ pint) mayonnaise
150 ml (¼ pint) soured cream

To serve:
nacho chips
shredded lettuce
hot tostada shells (optional)

Cut the turkey meat into long, generous pieces.

Bring a pan of water to the boil, add the green peppers and cook for 5 minutes, until they just start to soften – they must remain a very bright green. Drain the peppers well and, whilst still warm, purée them with the chillies, using a blender or food processor. It may need a little liquid – water or a little mayonnaise or soured cream will do. Then sieve the purée, using the back of a soup ladle to get a really smooth result.

Cut the papaya into generous strips or cubes. Mix gently and evenly with the turkey meat. Fold the mayonnaise and soured cream together, then blend in the green pepper sauce. Pour over the turkey and papaya, then cover and leave in the refrigerator or a cool place for 2 hours.

Serve lightly chilled but not directly from the refrigerator, with hot, crisp nacho chips or served on a bed of shredded lettuce on top of hot tostada shells (available from most supermarkets).

Serves 4

Goose and Celery Salad

300 g (10 oz) cold roast goose meat, skinned and shredded
1 crisp lettuce, separated into leaves
½ celery head, chopped
125 g (4 oz) shelled walnuts, chopped

Vinaigrette Dressing:
150 ml (¼ pint) olive oil
juice of 1 lemon
salt and pepper

To make the dressing, put the ingredients, with salt and pepper to taste, in a screw-top jar and shake until well mixed.

Mix together the goose meat and dressing and leave in the refrigerator or a cool place to marinate for 1 hour.

Arrange the lettuce leaves in a salad bowl. Add the celery and walnuts, pile the dressed goose on top and serve.

Serves 6

Goose and Red Cabbage Salad

250 g (8 oz) red cabbage, cored and
   shredded
300 g (10 oz) cold roast goose meat,
   skinned and shredded
1 teaspoon caraway seeds
Vinaigrette Dressing:
150 ml (¼ pint) olive oil
juice of 1 lemon
salt and pepper

Bring a large saucepan of salted
water to the boil and add the red
cabbage. Cover and quickly return
to the boil. Boil for 2 minutes, then
tip into a colander and refresh
under cold running water.
Drain well.

To make the dressing, put the
ingredients, with salt and pepper to
taste, in a screw-top jar and shake
until well mixed.

Pour the dressing over the
cabbage and leave to marinate for
1 hour. Fold in the goose and
caraway seeds and serve.

Serves 4

left: goose and celery salad
*above: goose, rice and mushroom
salad*

Goose, Rice and Mushroom Salad

300 g (10 oz) cold roast goose meat,
   skinned and shredded
375 g (12 oz) cold cooked long-grain
   rice
250 g (8 oz) mushrooms, sliced
6–8 spring onions, sliced
1 tablespoon Worcestershire sauce
150 ml (¼ pint) olive oil
juice of 1 lemon
salt and pepper

Mix all the ingredients together,
season to taste, and leave to stand
in a cool place for 1 hour, tossing
from time to time, before serving.

Serves 4–6

St Clements Goose Salad

2 oranges, peeled and segmented
2 tablespoons raisins
juice of 2 lemons
2 ripe avocados, peeled, pitted and
   sliced
300 g (10 oz) cold roast goose meat,
   skinned and shredded
salt and pepper

Marinate the orange segments and
raisins in the lemon juice for
1 hour. Fold in the avocado slices.
Season the goose with salt and
pepper to taste, add to the avocado
mixture and serve.

Serves 4

Duck, Mandarin and Rice Salad

2 egg yolks
175 g (6 oz) can mandarin orange
   segments in syrup
175 ml (6 fl oz) olive oil
300 g (10 oz) cold cooked rice
375 g (12 oz) cold roast duck meat,
   shredded
salt and pepper

Beat the egg yolks with about
3 tablespoons of the syrup from the
oranges to flavour. Season with salt
and pepper to taste and then add
the oil slowly in a thin stream,
beating all the time, to make an
orange-flavoured mayonnaise. If the
mayonnaise is really thick, add
more of the syrup to thin it.

   Mix the drained mandarin
segments with the rice and duck,
lightly fold in the orange
mayonnaise and serve.

Serves 4–6

Duck, Pasta and Parmesan Salad

375 g (12 oz) cooked pasta
2 tablespoons olive oil
375 g (12 oz) cold roast duck meat,
   shredded
150 g (5 oz) Parmesan cheese, grated
salt and pepper
chopped parsley, to garnish

Toss the pasta with the oil, then
fold in the remaining ingredients
and season with salt and pepper to
taste. Add more oil if necessary.
Garnish with a sprinkling of
chopped parsley before serving.

Serves 4

Variation:

Add to the salad 3 plum tomatoes,
seeded and chopped, about 8 black
olives, pitted, and a bunch of rocket and
watercress, divided into small sprigs.

Duck, Pepper and Pea Salad

375 g (12 oz) cold roast duck meat,
   shredded
250 g (8 oz) green peas, cooked
1 large green pepper, cored,
   deseeded and chopped
3 tablespoons Vinaigrette Dressing
   (see page 35)
1 tablespoon chopped mint

Mix together the shredded duck,
peas, green pepper and vinaigrette
dressing. Sprinkle with the chopped
mint.

   Leave the salad to stand in a cool
place for 1 hour before serving.

Serves 4

*right: duck, pasta and parmesan
salad; duck, pepper and pea salad;
duck, mandarin and rice salad*

Family Main Meals

Zitone Pesaro Style

175 g (6 oz) turkey breast meat

2 chicken livers

125 g (4 oz) ham

50 g (2 oz) mushrooms

125 g (4 oz) butter

1 small onion, chopped

7 tablespoons dry white wine

pinch of grated nutmeg

7 tablespoons cream

325 g (11 oz) zitone (pasta tubes)

75 g (3 oz) Gruyère cheese, grated

salt and pepper

Butter a baking dish. Mince the turkey, chicken livers, ham and mushrooms together. Melt 2 tablespoons of the butter in a heavy pan, add the onion and fry gently until golden. Stir in the minced mixture and cook, stirring, for 10 minutes.

Add the wine and simmer gently until it has evaporated by half, then add the nutmeg and salt and pepper to taste. Transfer to a bowl and stir in a little of the cream.

Cook the zitone in plenty of boiling salted water according to the directions on the packet. Drain thoroughly, then fill the tubes with the turkey mixture.

Arrange the stuffed zitone in two layers in the baking dish, covering each layer with the remaining cream and the Gruyère. Dot with the butter. Bake in a preheated oven, 200°C (400°F), Gas Mark 6, for 15 minutes. Serve at once.

Serves 4

Chicken, Walnut and Lemon Pancakes

Pancake Batter:

125 g (4 oz) plain flour

1 egg

300 ml (½ pint) milk

1 tablespoon oil

salt

oil, for cooking

Filling:

25 g (1 oz) butter

25 g (1 oz) plain flour

300 ml (½ pint) milk

finely grated rind of 1 lemon

250 g (8 oz) cooked chicken, chopped

40 g (1½ oz) shelled walnuts, coarsely chopped

1 tablespoon lemon juice

salt and pepper

To garnish:

chopped walnuts

lemon slices

Grease an ovenproof dish. Put the batter ingredients in a blender or food processor and blend together. Heat a little oil in a small crêpe or omelette pan. Pour in about 2 tablespoons of the batter. Cook on each side until golden. Repeat with the rest of the batter to make 8 pancakes. Stack the pancakes between greaseproof paper.

For the filling, melt the butter in a pan. Add the flour and cook for 1 minute. Gradually add the milk, blending well. Bring to the boil and cook for 2–3 minutes, stirring constantly. Remove 4 tablespoons of the sauce and set aside.

Add the lemon rind, chicken, walnuts and salt and pepper to taste to the sauce, blending well.

Fill each pancake with an equal quantity of this filling and roll up. Place the pancakes in the dish. Mix the reserved sauce with the lemon juice and salt and pepper to taste and spoon over the pancakes. Cover with foil and bake in a preheated oven, 190°C (375°F), Gas Mark 4, for 20 minutes. Serve hot, sprinkled with chopped walnuts and garnished with lemon slices.

Serves 4

right: chicken and rice ring

Chicken and Rice Ring

6 tablespoons mayonnaise

2 tablespoons finely chopped onion

1 tablespoon finely chopped tarragon

1 tablespoon finely chopped
watercress

125 g (4 oz) long-grain rice, cooked

50 g (2 oz) cooked sweetcorn kernels

1 small red pepper, cored, deseeded
and chopped

1 small green pepper, cored,
deseeded and chopped

250 g (8 oz) cooked chicken, chopped

125 g (4 oz) seedless green grapes,
halved

salt and pepper

tarragon or watercress sprigs, to
garnish

Oil a ring mould. Mix the
mayonnaise with the onion,
tarragon, watercress and salt and
pepper to taste.

Place 3 tablespoons of this
dressing in a bowl and mix with the
rice, sweetcorn and red and green
peppers. Spoon the rice mixture
into the ring mould and chill in the
refrigerator for about 1 hour until
it is firm.

Meanwhile, mix the chicken with
the grapes and remaining dressing.

To serve, invert the rice ring on to
a serving dish. Fill the centre with
the chicken mixture and garnish
with tarragon or watercress sprigs.

Serves 4–6

Cook's Tip:
Home-made mayonnaise

Home-made mayonnaise can be made
in a trice if prepared in a blender. For
about 300 ml (½ pint) mayonnaise, use
1 egg, 1 tablespoon vinegar, ½ teaspoon
salt, 1 teaspoon caster sugar with
mustard powder and pepper to taste.
Blend for 2–3 seconds to mix. With the
motor running, add about 300 ml
(½ pint) olive oil slowly through the feed
tube. The result is a deliciously thick and
creamy mayonnaise.

Chicken Risotto

3–4 tablespoons olive oil

1 celery stick, chopped

1 onion, finely chopped

1 carrot, diced

6 skinless, boneless chicken breasts, diced

7 tablespoons white wine

375 g (12 oz) tomatoes, skinned and mashed

300 ml (½ pint) hot chicken stock

500 g (1 lb) arborio or risotto rice

75 g (3 oz) butter, softened

75 g (3 oz) Parmesan cheese, grated

salt and pepper

Heat the oil in a large heavy pan, add the vegetables and fry gently until lightly coloured. Add the chicken and fry for a further 5 minutes, stirring constantly, then add the wine and boil until it has evaporated.

Add the tomatoes and salt and pepper. Cover and cook gently for 20 minutes, adding a little of the chicken stock if the mixture becomes dry.

Stir in the rice, then add some of the hot chicken stock. Cook over a low heat for 20–25 minutes until the rice is just tender, adding a little more stock to moisten, as necessary.

Remove from the heat, add the butter and Parmesan and fold gently to mix. Adjust the seasoning, if necessary, and serve immediately.

Serves 6–8

Chicken with Saffron Rice and Mushrooms

50 g (2 oz) butter

1 x 1.5 kg (3 lb) chicken, quartered,
   or 4 chicken portions

125 g (4 oz) mushrooms, sliced

1 onion, chopped

300 ml (½ pint) water

125 g (4 oz) long-grain rice

2 tablespoons vegetable oil

pinch of saffron threads

salt and pepper

Melt the butter in a saucepan. Add
the chicken pieces and fry until
lightly browned on all sides. Add
the mushrooms, onion, water and
salt and pepper. Cover the pan and
simmer gently for 1 hour.

Meanwhile, cook the rice in
plenty of boiling salted water for
10 minutes. Drain well and fry
gently in the oil with the saffron for
6–7 minutes.

Pile the rice on to a warmed
serving dish, arrange the chicken
pieces and vegetables on top
and serve.

Serves 4

41

Chicken Curry

1 kg (2 lb) chicken pieces, skinned
4 tablespoons vegetable oil
2 onions, chopped

Marinade:
2 garlic cloves, chopped
5 cm (2 inch) piece of fresh root
ginger, peeled and chopped
1 teaspoon turmeric
2 teaspoons ground cumin
1 teaspoon chilli powder
1 teaspoon pepper
3 tablespoons finely chopped
   coriander leaves
500 g (1 lb) natural yogurt
salt

To garnish:
coriander sprigs
lime wedges

Put all the marinade ingredients in a large bowl and mix well. Add the chicken pieces, turn to coat, and leave in a cool place to marinate for 4 hours, turning the chicken occasionally.

Heat the oil in a pan, add the onions and fry until golden. Add the chicken and the marinade. Bring to simmering point, cover the pan and cook for about 30 minutes until the chicken is tender. Serve garnished with coriander sprigs and wedges of lime.

Serves 4

Coronation Chicken

The mayonnaise sauce is delicately flavoured with apricot purée, which is best made with dried apricots. If canned apricots are used, unless they are unsweetened, you will need extra lemon juice to counteract the sweetness.

1 cooked chicken, about 1.5 kg (3 lb), jointed, skinned and boned
1 tablespoon oil
1 small onion, chopped
1–2 teaspoons curry powder
2 teaspoons tomato purée
6 tablespoons dry white wine
4½ tablespoons chicken stock or water
1 teaspoon sugar
2–3 teaspoons lemon juice
300 ml (½ pint) mayonnaise
3 tablespoons apricot purée
2–3 tablespoons double cream, lightly whipped
salt and pepper
To garnish:
sliced apricots
watercress sprigs or black and green seedless grapes, halved
toasted flaked almonds

Cut the chicken into neat pieces and, if hot, leave in a cool place until cold.

Heat the oil and fry the onion gently until soft. Add the curry powder and tomato purée and fry, stirring, for a further 3 minutes. Stir in the wine and stock or water and cook, uncovered, for about 10 minutes. Add the sugar and lemon juice, and season with salt and pepper to taste.

Cool thoroughly, and then gradually stir the mixture into the mayonnaise. Add the apricot purée.

Stir the cream into the sauce, adjust the seasoning and mix in the chicken pieces. Spoon into a serving dish and chill in the refrigerator.

Garnish with apricots and watercress or grapes, scatter the top with flaked toasted almonds and serve, with a rice salad if liked.

Serves 4

Chicken Pilau

To prevent black rings forming around the yolks of the eggs, after cooking drain and leave in a saucepan under cold running water for about 2 minutes.

4 small onions, halved
2 bay leaves
1 litre (1¾ pints) water
2 kg (4 lb) chicken
½ teaspoon saffron threads
125 g (4 oz) ghee
5 garlic cloves, sliced
10 cloves
10 cardamom pods
2 x 7.5 cm (3 inch) cinnamon sticks
625 g (1¼ lb) basmati rice, washed
50 g (2 oz) blanched almonds
125 g (4 oz) sultanas
To garnish:
hard-boiled egg quarters
fried onion rings

Place the onion halves, bay leaves and water in a pan and bring to the boil. Add the chicken, cover and simmer for 1½–2 hours until tender. Remove the flesh from the chicken and cut into pieces; reserve the cooking liquid and onions.

Put the saffron in a cup and pour over a little boiling water. Leave to soak for 20 minutes.

Heat the ghee in a pan, add the reserved cooked onions, the garlic, cloves, cardamom and cinnamon sticks and fry for 5 minutes. Add the rice and enough reserved cooking liquid to cover the rice, then the strained saffron water. Cook, uncovered, for 10–15 minutes, then cover the pan and cook until the rice is tender and the liquid has been absorbed. Mix with the chicken, almonds and sultanas, and serve garnished with hard-boiled eggs and fried onion rings.

Serves 6

left: chicken curry

Tarragon Chicken

50 g (2 oz) butter
1 x 1.75 kg (3½ lb) chicken, skinned and jointed, or 4 chicken portions
2 onions, chopped
40 g (1½ oz) plain flour
2 tablespoons chopped tarragon
450 ml (¾ pint) chicken stock
salt and pepper

Melt the butter in a flameproof casserole. Add the chicken and onions and fry until the chicken has browned. Sprinkle over the flour and stir well. Continue to cook, allowing the flour mixture to colour lightly. Stir in 1 tablespoon of the tarragon together with the stock.

Bring to the boil and skim the surface. Season with salt and pepper. Cover and simmer gently for 1 hour until the chicken is cooked and tender. Just before serving, adjust the seasoning, if necessary, and sprinkle with the remaining tarragon.

Serves 4

Curried Chicken

Serve with poppadums, wholewheat chapatis or rice. A fruit chutney and side dishes of cucumber and grated carrot, also make good accompaniments.

2 tablespoons vegetable oil
½ teaspoon cumin seeds
½ teaspoon ground cinnamon
seeds from 2 cardamom pods, crushed
2 onions, chopped
1 heaped teaspoon chopped fresh root ginger
2 garlic cloves, crushed
3–4 skinless chicken breasts, cut into slivers
400 g (13 oz) can tomatoes
1 tablespoon soy sauce
1–2 teaspoons sugar
½ teaspoon garam masala
pepper

Heat the oil and fry the cumin seeds, cinnamon and cardamom seeds for 1 minute. Add the onions, ginger and garlic and fry for 2 minutes. Add the chicken pieces and stir-fry for about 5 minutes until lightly coloured. Add the tomatoes, with their juice, soy sauce and sugar to taste. Bring to the boil, lower the heat and stir in the garam masala. Season with pepper to taste. Serve at once.

Serves 4

left: tarragon chicken
right: chilli chicken

Chilli Chicken

Fresh red hot chillies are a major and important ingredient in this recipe both for their flavour and colour. They can be seeded before use to reduce their fieriness.

750 g (1½ lb) boneless chicken
   breasts, cubed
1 teaspoon sugar
3 red chillies
4 almonds
1 stem lemon grass, sliced
1 teaspoon fenugreek
2.5 cm (1 inch) piece of fresh root
   ginger, peeled
6 small red onions or shallots, sliced
4 garlic cloves, crushed
4 tablespoons vegetable oil
150 ml (¼ pint) water
salt
shredded spring onions, to garnish

Sprinkle the chicken with the sugar and set aside in a cool place. Purée the chillies with the almonds, lemon grass, fenugreek and half the ginger. Purée the remaining ginger with the onions or shallots and the crushed garlic.

Heat the oil and fry the chilli-spice mixture for 1–2 minutes. Add the onion mixture and fry for a further 1–2 minutes. Stir in the chicken pieces to coat with the spices then add the water and salt. Cover the pan and cook gently for 5 minutes. Adjust the seasoning, if necessary.

Transfer to a serving dish and garnish with the spring onions.

Serves 4

Coq au Vin

50 g (2 oz) butter

175 g (6 oz) piece collar bacon, diced (or bacon lardons)

2 onions, chopped

2 garlic cloves, crushed

2 kg (4 lb) chicken, skinned and jointed, or 4 chicken portions

50 g (2 oz) plain flour

150 ml (¼ pint) chicken stock

300 ml (½ pint) dry red wine

6–8 mushrooms, sliced

1 tablespoon tomato purée

1 bay leaf

salt and pepper

fried bread triangles, to garnish

Melt the butter in a flameproof casserole and fry the bacon, onions, garlic and chicken pieces until evenly browned.

Sprinkle over the flour and stir well. Cook until lightly coloured, then stir in the stock and wine.

Season with salt and pepper, then add the mushrooms, tomato purée and bay leaf. Cover and simmer gently for 1 hour.

Remove the bay leaf and adjust the seasoning if necessary. Serve garnished with fried bread triangles.

Serves 4

Chicken in Peanut Sauce

This dish is excellent served with plain boiled rice to bring out the nutty flavour of the sauce. Use crunchy peanut butter rather than the smooth variety.

1 x 1.75 kg (3½ lb) chicken, skinned and jointed, or 4 chicken portions

2 large onions, finely chopped

2 garlic cloves, crushed

125 g (4 oz) peanut butter

400 g (13 oz) can chopped tomatoes

1 teaspoon ground cinnamon

1 tablespoon ground cumin

1 teaspoon chilli powder

2 teaspoons paprika

2 teaspoons brown sugar

1 teaspoon salt

2 tablespoons lemon juice

1–2 sprigs coriander leaves, to garnish

Using a sharp knife, make a few diagonal cuts on the fleshy part of the chicken joints, then place them in an ovenproof casserole.

Mix together the remaining ingredients, except the coriander, in

a bowl and pour the sauce evenly over the chicken. Cover and bake in a preheated oven, 180°C (350°F), Gas Mark 4, for about 1–1½ hours until the chicken is tender. Stir the sauce and baste the chicken joints once during the cooking time. Garnish with the coriander sprigs and serve.

Serves 4

left: coq au vin
above: *chicken casserole with mushrooms*

Chicken Casserole with Mushrooms

50 g (2 oz) butter
1 x 2 kg (4 lb) chicken, skinned and
   jointed, or 4 chicken portions
1 onion, chopped
20 g (¾ oz) plain flour
300 ml (½ pint) chicken stock
250 g (8 oz) mushrooms, sliced
1 tablespoon soy sauce
2 teaspoons Worcestershire sauce
salt and pepper

Melt the butter in a flameproof casserole. Add the chicken and onion and fry until the chicken joints are browned. Sprinkle over the flour and cook, stirring, for 1 minute. Stir in the stock, then bring to the boil and skim.

Stir in the mushrooms, soy and Worcestershire sauces and salt and pepper. Cover and simmer gently for 1 hour until the chicken is tender. Adjust the seasoning before serving.

Serves 4

Madras Curry

50 g (2 oz) butter or margarine
1 x 1.5 kg (3 lb) chicken, jointed or
   4 chicken portions
2 onions, chopped
50 g (2 oz) hot curry powder
2 garlic cloves, chopped
900 ml (1½ pints) chicken stock
juice of ½ lemon
2 tablespoons tomato purée
1 tablespoon demerara sugar
2 bay leaves
salt and pepper

Melt the butter or margarine in a flameproof casserole and fry the chicken pieces, onions and curry powder together until the chicken is evenly browned. Add the garlic, then stir in the stock, lemon juice, tomato purée, sugar and bay leaves. Season with salt and pepper, then cover the casserole and simmer gently for 1½ hours.

   Remove the bay leaves and adjust the seasoning if necessary. Serve the curry with plain boiled rice, poppadums, coconut, chutney and hot pickles.

Serves 4

Chicken Casserole with Tomatoes and Celery

50 g (2 oz) butter
1 x 1.75 kg (3½ lb) chicken, quartered,
   or 4 chicken portions
2 onions, chopped
2 garlic cloves, crushed
1 celery head, cut into 2.5 cm
   (1 inch) pieces
1 tablespoon dried basil
400 g (13 oz) can tomatoes
salt and pepper

Melt the butter in a flameproof casserole and fry the chicken, onions and garlic until the chicken is browned. Add the celery, basil and canned tomatoes with their juice and season with salt and pepper to taste.

   Cover and transfer to a preheated oven, 180°C (350°F), Gas Mark 4. Cook for 1½ hours. Adjust the seasoning, if necessary, before serving.

Serves 4

Chicken Provençal

125 ml (4 fl oz) olive oil
1 x 1.75 kg (3½ lb) chicken, quartered,
   or 4 chicken portions
2 onions, chopped
2 garlic cloves, crushed
2 green peppers, cored, deseeded
   and finely diced
150 ml (¼ pint) dry white wine
6 tomatoes, skinned and chopped
1 tablespoon tomato purée
1 bay leaf
1 teaspoon dried oregano
salt and pepper

Heat the oil in a flameproof casserole and fry the chicken, onions, garlic and green peppers until the chicken is browned. Add the wine, tomatoes, tomato purée, bay leaf and oregano. Season with salt and pepper, then cover and simmer gently for 1¼ hours.

   Just before serving, remove the bay leaf and adjust the seasoning, if necessary. Serve with saffron rice.

Serves 4

right: madras curry; chicken casserole with tomatoes and celery; chicken provençal

Chicken Chasseur

50 g (2 oz) butter

1 x 1.75 kg (3½ lb) chicken, jointed

6 streaky bacon rashers, rinds removed, cut into 4 pieces

2 onions, finely chopped

50 g (2 oz) plain flour

150 ml (¼ pint) dry red wine

600 ml (1 pint) chicken stock

3 tomatoes, skinned and chopped

250 g (8 oz) mushrooms, sliced

2 bay leaves

1 tablespoon soy sauce

salt and pepper

Melt the butter in a flameproof casserole and fry the chicken pieces with the bacon and onions until the chicken is browned.

Sprinkle the flour into the casserole and cook, stirring, for 1 minute. Stir in the wine and stock. Bring to the boil and skim. Add the tomatoes, mushrooms, bay leaves, soy sauce and salt and pepper to taste.

Cover and simmer gently for 1 hour. Remove the bay leaves and adjust the seasoning, if necessary before serving.

Serves 4

Jugged Chicken

1 x 1.5 kg (3 lb) chicken, skinned and quartered, or 4 chicken portions

150 ml (¼ pint) dry red wine

2 onions, chopped

2 garlic cloves, crushed

2 bay leaves

50 g (2 oz) margarine

50 g (2 oz) plain flour

600 ml (1 pint) chicken stock

1 tablespoon tomato purée

1 tablespoon dried tarragon

4 tablespoons port wine

salt and pepper

Put the chicken pieces into a bowl and pour over the red wine. Add the onions, garlic and bay leaves. Leave in the refrigerator or a cool place to marinate overnight.

Remove the chicken from the marinade and pat dry with kitchen paper. Melt the margarine in a flameproof casserole, then add the chicken pieces and fry until lightly browned on all sides. Sprinkle the flour into the casserole and cook, stirring, until light brown. Stir in the marinade, stock, tomato purée, salt and pepper and tarragon. Cover and simmer for 1 hour.

Stir in the port, remove the bay leaves and adjust the seasoning, if necessary. Serve from the casserole.

Serves 4

left: jugged chicken
right: chicken with herbs

Chicken with Herbs

50 g (2 oz) butter

1 x 1.75 kg (3½ lb) chicken, quartered, or 4 chicken portions

125 g (4 oz) smoked bacon, rinds removed, finely diced

1 onion, chopped

50 g (2 oz) plain flour

600 ml (1 pint) chicken stock

1 tablespoon chopped parsley, plus extra to garnish

1 tablespoon chopped chives

1 tablespoon chopped tarragon

1 tablespoon chopped chervil

2 tablespoons double cream

salt and pepper

Melt the butter in a flameproof casserole and add the chicken pieces, bacon and onion. Fry until the chicken pieces are lightly browned on all sides. Sprinkle over the flour and cook, stirring, for 1 minute. Stir in the stock, then bring to the boil and skim. Cover and simmer gently for 30 minutes.

Add 1½ teaspoons of the chopped parsley and all the remaining herbs. Cover and simmer for a further 20 minutes. Season to taste.

When the chicken is tender, stir in the cream and remaining parsley and serve, sprinkled with parsley.

Serves 4

Roast Chicken with Green Butter Sauce

1 x 1.75 kg (3½ lb) chicken
50 g (2 oz) butter, melted
1 tablespoon plain flour
salt and pepper
Sauce:
50 g (2 oz) butter

1 bunch of watercress, chopped
1 tablespoon chopped tarragon
1 tablespoon chopped parsley
2 tablespoons chopped spinach
1 tablespoon chopped sorrel
   (optional)

Season the chicken with salt and pepper. Brush with the melted butter and sprinkle with the flour. Put in a roasting tin and roast in a preheated oven, 200°C (400°F), Gas Mark 6, for about 1¼ hours. Remove from the oven and keep hot on a warmed dish.

To make the sauce, add the butter to the roasting tin. Stir in the remaining sauce ingredients and heat gently, stirring. If the sauce is too dry, add a little chicken stock to moisten it. Season with salt and pepper to taste. Carve the chicken and serve with the sauce.

Serves 4

Chicken with Olives

50 g (2 oz) butter

1 x 1.5 kg (3 lb) chicken, skinned and
  cut into small pieces

1 onion, chopped

1 garlic clove, crushed

600 ml (1 pint) chicken stock

1 thyme sprig

2 teaspoons arrowroot

1½ tablespoons water

150 g (5 oz) jar stuffed green olives,
  drained

salt and pepper

Melt the butter in a saucepan and fry the chicken pieces, onion and garlic until the chicken is lightly browned. Stir in the stock and bring to the boil. Skim and then add the thyme and salt and pepper. Cover and simmer gently for 1 hour.

Transfer the chicken pieces to a warmed serving dish and keep hot. Dissolve the arrowroot in the water and add to the liquid in the saucepan. Simmer, stirring, until thickened. Stir in the olives and heat through. Adjust the seasoning, if necessary, then pour the sauce over the chicken pieces and serve.

Serves 4

left: roast chicken with green butter sauce
right: chicken with olives

Chicken Mornay

75 g (3 oz) butter

1 x 1.75 kg (3½ lb) chicken, jointed

40 g (1½ oz) plain flour

300 ml (½ pint) dry white wine

300 ml (½ pint) chicken stock

1 garlic clove, crushed

1 thyme sprig

125 g (4 oz) cheese, grated

2 egg yolks

2 tablespoons double cream

salt and pepper

Melt 50 g (2 oz) of the butter in a saucepan. Add the chicken pieces and fry lightly until golden. Sprinkle 25 g (1 oz) of the flour into the pan and cook, stirring, for 1 minute. Stir in the wine, stock and garlic. Bring to the boil and skim the surface. Add the thyme and salt and pepper.

Simmer gently for 1 hour until the chicken is cooked. Transfer the chicken to a flameproof serving dish and keep hot.

Remove the thyme. Mix the remaining butter and flour together to make a paste. Add this in small pieces to the sauce, stirring well, and cook until thickened. Stir in 75 g (3 oz) of the cheese and remove the pan from the heat.

Beat together the egg yolks and cream and beat into the sauce. Taste and adjust the seasoning, if necessary. Pour over the chicken, then sprinkle with the remaining grated cheese and brown quickly under a preheated hot grill before serving.

Serves 4

Casserole of Chicken in Beer

50 g (2 oz) butter

1 x 1.5 kg (3 lb) chicken, quartered,
   or 4 chicken portions

2 onions, chopped

2 garlic cloves, crushed

900 ml (1½ pints) light beer or lager

50 g (2 oz) plain flour

175 g (6 oz) mushrooms, sliced

2 tablespoons tomato purée

1 bay leaf

salt and pepper

chopped parsley, to garnish

Melt the butter in a flameproof
casserole. Add the chicken quarters,
onions and garlic and fry until the
chicken pieces are browned all over.

Meanwhile, boil the beer in
another pan until reduced to
600 ml (1 pint).

Sprinkle the flour over the
chicken pieces and cook, stirring,
for 1 minute. Stir in the hot beer
then bring to the boil and skim the
surface. Cover and simmer for
10 minutes, then stir in the
mushrooms, tomato purée, bay leaf
and salt and pepper.

Simmer for about 1 hour until
the chicken is tender. Remove the
bay leaf and adjust the seasoning,
if necessary. Serve garnished
with parsley.

Serves 4

Chicken Casseroled with Lemon and Chives

50 g (2 oz) butter

1 x 1.5 kg (3 lb) chicken, quartered,
   or 4 chicken portions

150 ml (¼ pint) dry white wine

150 ml (¼ pint) water

thinly pared rind and juice of 1 lemon

3 tablespoons chopped chives or
   green spring onion tops

2 teaspoons arrowroot

1 tablespoon water

salt and pepper

Melt the butter in a saucepan. Add
the chicken quarters and brown on
all sides. Add the wine, water, pared
lemon rind and juice. Bring to the
boil and skim. Season with salt and
pepper, then cover and simmer
gently for 1 hour.

Ten minutes before the chicken is
ready, add 2 tablespoons of the
chives or spring onions.

Transfer the chicken pieces to a
warmed dish and keep hot. Dissolve
the arrowroot in the water and add
to the sauce in the saucepan. Bring
to the boil, stirring until thickened.

Adjust the seasoning, then pour
the sauce over the chicken pieces.
Serve sprinkled with the remaining
chives or spring onions.

Serves 4

Chicken in Cider with Apples

1 x 1.5 kg (3 lb) chicken, quartered,
   or 4 chicken portions

3 large cooking apples, peeled, cored
   and finely chopped

600 ml (1 pint) dry cider

2 bay leaves

50 g (2 oz) butter, diced

salt and pepper

lemon slices, to garnish

Put the chicken quarters into a
saucepan that will just hold them
comfortably. Pack the apples around
the chicken to fill the pan almost
completely. Pour over the cider to
cover. Add the bay leaves and salt
and pepper and then top with the
diced butter.

Cover the pan and bring to the
boil. Reduce the heat and simmer
gently for about 1 hour until the
chicken is cooked.

Transfer the chicken to a warmed
serving dish and keep hot. Remove
the bay leaves. Sieve the apples and
cooking liquid, or purée using a
blender or food processor. Adjust
the seasoning, if necessary, and
pour over the chicken. Serve
garnished with lemon slices.

Serves 4

right: chicken casseroled with lemon and chives

Spicy Chicken

8 chicken pieces, skinned

juice of 1 lemon

4 tablespoons coconut milk or 4 tablespoons desiccated coconut, soaked in 4 tablespoons hot water

2–4 red chillies, deseeded chopped

4 small onions, quartered

2 garlic cloves

4 Brazil nuts, shelled

1 cm (½ inch) piece of fresh root ginger, peeled

1 teaspoon grated lemon rind

1 teaspoon shrimp paste (*Terasi*)

1 teaspoon sugar

3 tablespoons vegetable oil

300 ml (½ pint) water

salt

Rub the chicken pieces with the lemon juice and leave in a cool place for 20 minutes.

Put all the remaining ingredients, except the oil and water, in a blender or food processor and mix to a smooth paste. Heat the oil in a large pan and fry the paste, stirring, for 5 minutes.

Add the chicken and fry for a further 5 minutes. Stir in the water and cook, uncovered, for 30 minutes until the chicken is tender and the sauce is thick. Serve immediately.

Serves 4

left: grilled chicken with warm aïoli
right: chicken with chestnuts

Grilled Chicken with Warm Aïoli

1 x 1.5 kg (3 lb) chicken, quartered, or 4 chicken portions

40 g (1½ oz) butter, melted

50 g (2 oz) plain flour

lemon wedges, to garnish

Aïoli (garlic mayonnaise):

2 egg yolks

15 g (½ oz) sugar

juice of 1 lemon

300 ml (½ pint) olive oil

3 garlic cloves, crushed

1 tablespoon boiling water

salt and pepper

Brush the chicken with the melted butter and dust with the flour. Cook under a preheated medium grill for 15–16 minutes on each side until brown and tender.

Meanwhile, make the aïoli. Beat the egg yolks, salt and pepper, sugar and lemon juice in a heatproof bowl. Gradually beat in the oil in drops, until the mayonnaise thickens. When half the oil has been added, add the remainder in a thin stream. Mix in the garlic and beat in the boiling water. Adjust the seasoning. Stand the bowl in hot water to heat through gently.

Arrange the chicken on a warmed serving dish and coat with the aïoli. Garnish with lemon wedges.

Serves 4

Chicken with Chestnuts

500 g (1 lb) chestnuts
50 g (2 oz) butter
1 x 1.5 kg (3 lb) chicken, quartered or
  4 chicken portions
2 onions, chopped
600 ml (1 pint) chicken stock
50 g (2 oz) plain flour
250 g (8 oz) button mushrooms
salt and pepper
orange slices, to garnish

With a sharp knife, make an incision in each chestnut and put them into a saucepan of cold water. Bring to the boil, then reduce the heat and simmer for 10 minutes. Drain the chestnuts and peel off both the outer and inner skins, then poach in the stock for 25 minutes. Drain, reserving the stock.

Meanwhile, melt the butter in a flameproof casserole. Add the chicken and onions and fry until the chicken pieces are lightly browned on all sides.

Sprinkle the chicken with the flour and cook, stirring, for 1 minute. Add the stock from the chestnuts and bring to the boil, stirring. Season with salt and pepper and add the mushrooms. Cover the pan and simmer for 1 hour.

Ten minutes before serving, add the reserved chestnuts and heat through. Serve garnished with orange slices.

Serves 4

Roast Farmhouse Chicken

1 x 1.75–2 kg (3½–4 lb) chicken with giblets

1 quantity Orange Stuffing (see page 70)

125 g (4 oz) streaky bacon rashers

2–3 tablespoons chicken fat, unsalted butter or margarine

watercress sprigs, to garnish

Giblet Stock:

1 small onion, peeled

1 sprig each thyme and parsley

1 bay leaf

salt and pepper

Grease a roasting tin well. To make the giblet stock, clean the giblets under running cold water, then put into a saucepan of cold water with the onion, herbs and seasoning. Cover and simmer gently for about 1½ hours.

Fill the neck end of the chicken with the stuffing. Truss neatly and place the chicken in the roasting tin. Remove the rind from the bacon rashers and use to cover the chicken breast. Spread the fat over the legs and cover the chicken with greased greaseproof paper or foil.

Roast in a preheated oven, 200°C (400°F), Gas Mark 6, for 1 hour, then remove the paper or foil. Set the bacon aside and keep warm. Baste the chicken with the fat in the pan and return to the oven for a

further 15 minutes to brown.

To test if the chicken is ready, insert a skewer into the thickest part of the inside leg and press out a little of the juice – it should be amber coloured.

Remove the chicken to a heated carving dish and keep warm. Slowly pour the fat out of the roasting tin, leaving the residue and juices in the bottom. Add 300–450 ml (½–¾ pint) giblet stock to the tin and boil briskly to reduce it, scraping the residue up from the bottom. When the gravy is well coloured, season to taste with salt and pepper and pour it into a warm sauce boat.

Arrange the crisped bacon rashers around the chicken and garnish with fresh watercress sprigs. Serve with the gravy, roast or baked potatoes and cauliflower or leeks. Pork chipolata sausages can be baked in the oven for the last 20 minutes of the cooking time and arranged around the serving dish with the bacon.

Serves 4–5

West Country Chicken with Cider

This is a typical West Country dish with its cider, cream and apples. The meat from the carcass and giblets together with stock will make a tasty risotto which can be served the next day.

1 x 1.75 kg (3½ lb) chicken, jointed
flour, for coating
Sauce:
75 g (3 oz) unsalted butter
1 large onion, thinly sliced
2 celery sticks, chopped
1 large or 2 small cooking apples
25 g (1 oz) flour
150 ml (¼ pint) cider
300 ml (½ pint) chicken stock
2–4 tablespoons double cream
salt and pepper
To garnish:
fried apple rings
celery leaves

Coat the chicken joints lightly with flour, patting off any surplus. Heat two-thirds of the butter in a flameproof casserole or sauté pan and fry the chicken joints briskly until browned all over. Remove the chicken, add the onion and celery to the pan and fry gently until soft.

Peel, core and roughly chop the apples. Add to the pan and fry gently until well buttered. Remove the pan from the heat and stir in the flour to absorb the fat. Gradually stir in the cider and chicken stock.

Bring to simmering point, add the chicken and a little more stock, if necessary, to cover the joints. Cover the pan and simmer gently for 30 minutes until the chicken juices run clear.

Remove the chicken, arrange on a heated serving plate and keep warm. Stir the double cream into the sauce in the pan and cook over a low heat for 2–3 minutes. Season to taste with salt and pepper.

Serve the chicken with the sauce, garnished with fried apple rings and celery leaves.

Serves 4

Roast Chicken with Pork and Herb Stuffing

1 x 1.75 kg (3½ lb) chicken
50 g (2 oz) butter, melted
watercress sprigs, to garnish
Pork and Herb Stuffing:
25 g (1 oz) butter
1 onion, chopped
125 g (4 oz) pork sausagemeat
75 g (3 oz) fresh breadcrumbs
2 teaspoons chopped mixed herbs
1 egg, beaten
salt and pepper

To make the stuffing, melt the butter in a frying pan and fry the onion until it is soft but not brown. Mix in the sausagemeat, breadcrumbs and herbs. Remove from the heat and allow to cool, then stir in the beaten egg and salt and pepper to taste. Use to stuff the neck end of the chicken.

Truss the chicken, place in a roasting pan and brush with the melted butter. Season generously with salt and pepper. Roast in a preheated oven, 180°C (350°F), Gas Mark 4, for about 1 hour basting once or twice, until tender and golden. Serve garnished with watercress sprigs.

Serves 4

above left: roast chicken with pork and herb stuffing

Chicken Liver Kebabs

Nowadays chicken livers can be bought in convenient packs of 250 g (8 oz) and 500 g (1 lb). The livers should always be carefully cleaned and never overcooked, otherwise these tender morsels will become hard.

4 chicken livers, cleaned and halved
2 tablespoons butter
4–8 bacon rolls
8 mushroom caps
4 wedges green pepper
4–8 cocktail sausages
oil, for brushing
dried mixed herbs
salt and pepper

Fry the halved chicken livers in butter until just stiffened. Thread on to 4 skewers with the bacon rolls, mushrooms, green pepper and sausages, alternating the colours. Brush with oil, season well and sprinkle with herbs (or baste with barbecue sauce).

Cook under a preheated hot grill or over a charcoal grill, turning frequently, for about 10 minutes until the livers, bacon and sausages are cooked and the vegetables are slightly charred.

Serves 2

Variation:
Small chunks of chicken can be used instead of livers. Button onions, red and yellow peppers and pineapple wedges are attractive additions to the skewers.

Barbecued Chicken

The bed of charcoal should be shallow so that it is easy to control. Do not poke the charcoal during cooking because this will slow down the fire, not brighten it.

Serve the chicken with baked potatoes, sweetcorn or roasted peppers and foil-baked peas and beans. Alternatively, opt for garlic bread and bowls of cucumber and tomato salad and tossed green salad with vinaigrette dressing.

4 chicken quarters
Barbecue Sauce:
2 tablespoons oil
1 onion, finely chopped
2 garlic cloves, crushed
200 g (7 oz) can chopped tomatoes
2 tablespoons tomato purée
1 tablespoon light brown sugar
1 tablespoon Worcestershire sauce
few drops Tabasco sauce

2 tablespoons white wine vinegar
1 tablespoon English mustard
salt and pepper

To make the barbecue sauce, heat the oil in a saucepan, add the onion and garlic and fry for 7–8 minutes, stirring occasionally, until the onion is soft and lightly browned.

Add the remaining ingredients to the pan and simmer gently for about 10 minutes, stirring occasionally, until the sauce has thickened slightly.

To make a smooth sauce, if preferred, tip into a blender or food processor and blend for a few seconds. Adjust the seasoning, if necessary. Leave to cool.

Using a sharp knife, cut 2 parallel, deep slashes in the thickest part of each chicken portion. Spread some of the sauce liberally over each portion, making sure that it goes well into the slashes. Cover and leave in a cool place for 2 hours.

Oil the barbecue rack. Put the chicken portions on the rack and cook over a preheated barbecue for about 25 minutes, basting occasionally with the sauce and turning the portions over regularly. Alternatively, bake in a preheated oven, 190°C (375°F), Gas Mark 5, for 40–45 minutes.

Serves 4

left: chicken liver kebabs
right: chicken maryland

Chicken Maryland

25 g (1 oz) plain flour
1 x 1.5 kg (3 lb) chicken, skinned and quartered, or 4 chicken portions
2 eggs
150 ml (¼ pint) milk
175–250 g (6–8 oz) dried breadcrumbs
2 bananas, halved
oil, for deep frying
250 g (8 oz) can sweetcorn
salt and pepper
parsley sprigs, to garnish

Mix the flour with salt and pepper and sift over the chicken. Beat the eggs and milk together and dip the floured chicken pieces into the beaten egg mixture before coating them evenly with breadcrumbs. Do the same with the halved bananas.

Deep-fry the chicken portions in the oil for 12–15 minutes, then drain them on kitchen paper and keep hot while frying the breaded banana halves for 3–4 minutes.

Meanwhile, in a small saucepan, gently heat the sweetcorn. Drain and serve the sweetcorn with the fried chicken portions and breaded bananas and garnish with sprigs of parsley.

Serves 4

Grilled Anchovy Chicken

1 x 1.5 kg (3 lb) chicken, quartered,
  or 4 chicken portions
40 g (1½ oz) butter, melted
50 g (2 oz) plain flour
salt and pepper
parsley sprigs, to garnish
Anchovy Sauce:
25 g (1 oz) butter
25 g (1 oz) plain flour
300 ml (½ pint) milk
2 tablespoons anchovy essence
1 tablespoon tomato purée
juice of 1 lemon
50 g (2 oz) can anchovy fillets, with
  their oil, chopped

Brush the chicken portions with the melted butter, season with salt and pepper, and dust with the flour. Cook under a preheated medium grill for 15–16 minutes on each side until brown and tender. Keep hot.

To make the sauce, melt the butter in a saucepan. Add the flour and cook, stirring, for 1 minute. Gradually stir in the milk and bring to the boil, stirring. Simmer until thickened. Beat in the anchovy essence, tomato purée, lemon juice and anchovies with their oil. Heat through gently and add a little salt and pepper to taste.

Arrange the chicken on a warmed serving dish and coat with the sauce. Garnish with parsley sprigs.

Serves 4

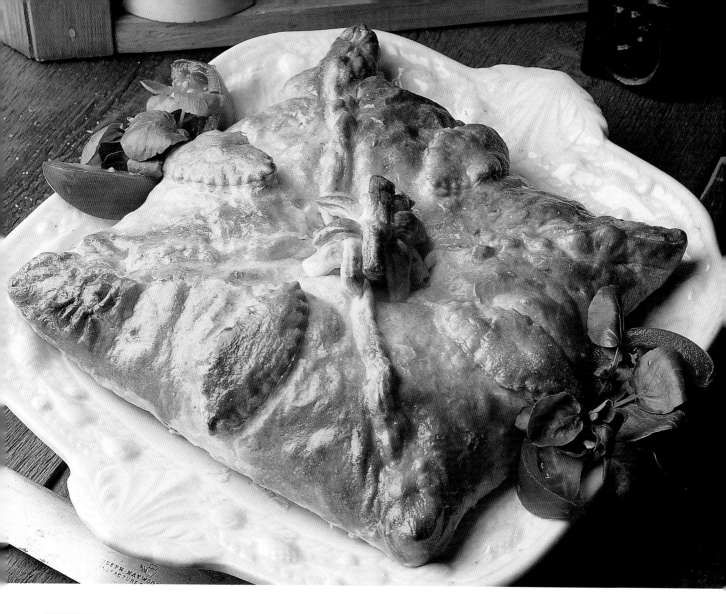

Chicken and Ham Pie

125–150 g (4–5 oz) cooked chicken, chopped

50 g (2 oz) cooked ham, diced

150 g (5 oz) Cheddar cheese, diced

50 g (2 oz) mushrooms, chopped

1 tablespoon chopped parsley

1 egg

250 g (8 oz) puff pastry, defrosted, if frozen

salt and pepper

beaten egg, to glaze

To garnish:

tomato quarters

watercress sprigs

Mix together the chicken, ham, cheese, mushrooms and parsley. Season to taste. Beat the egg and stir into the mixture.

Roll out the pastry thinly into a 38 x 25 cm (15 x 10 inches) rectangle. Cut out a 25 cm (10 inch) square and place on a baking tray. Pile the filling in the centre. Fold the corners of the square to the centre and seal with beaten egg. Brush more egg evenly over the pie. Open the outer corners slightly to allow steam to escape from the pie during cooking.

Use the remaining pastry to make decorations, glaze with egg and arrange on the pie. Bake in a preheated oven, 220°C (425°F), Gas Mark 7, for 25 minutes, until well risen and golden brown. Serve hot garnished with tomato quarters and watercress sprigs.

Serves 4–6

Chicken and Mushroom Pie

50 g (2 oz) butter
1 x 1.75 kg (3½ lb) chicken, cut into
  8 pieces
1 large onion, chopped
40 g (1½ oz) plain flour
300 ml (½ pint) chicken stock
1 bay leaf
175 g (6 oz) mushrooms, sliced
250 g (8 oz) puff pastry, defrosted, if
  frozen
1 egg, beaten
salt and pepper

Melt the butter in a saucepan. Add the chicken and onion and fry until lightly browned. Sprinkle over the flour and cook, stirring, for 1 minute. Stir in the stock. Bring to the boil and skim. Season with salt and pepper and add the bay leaf, then simmer for 1 hour until the chicken is tender. Remove the bay leaf and set aside to cool.

Stir in the mushrooms and transfer to a pie dish. Roll out the puff pastry and use to cover the dish. Make a hole in the centre and decorate with the pastry trimmings.

Brush with the beaten egg and bake in a preheated oven, 200°C (400°F), Gas Mark 6, for 40 minutes until the pastry is crisp and golden.

Serves 4

Turkey and Gammon Pie

50 g (2 oz) butter
2 onions, minced
2 garlic cloves, crushed
500 g (1 lb) turkey meat, finely diced
250 g (8 oz) gammon, finely diced
40 g (1½ oz) plain flour
600 ml (1 pint) turkey or chicken
  stock
250 g (8 oz) mushrooms, sliced
250 g (8 oz) puff pastry, defrosted, if
  frozen
1 egg, beaten
salt and pepper

Melt the butter in a saucepan and fry the onions and garlic until soft but not brown. Add the turkey and gammon. Sprinkle with the flour and cook, stirring, for 2 minutes. Stir in the stock and season with salt and pepper to taste. Remove from the heat and add the mushrooms. Turn into a 1.2 litre (2 pint) pie dish and allow to cool.

Cover the dish with puff pastry, make a hole in the centre and decorate with the pastry trimmings. Brush with beaten egg and bake in a preheated oven, 200°C (400°F), Gas Mark 6, for 30 minutes. Reduce the heat to 180°C (350°F), Gas Mark 4 and bake for a further 30 minutes. If the pastry gets too brown, cover it with damp greaseproof paper.

Serves 6

Viennese Turkey Escalopes

Commercial turkey steaks are cut by machine from raw turkey breasts. A very sharp knife and considerable skill would be required to produce them at home. They make an excellent substitute for veal in this classic dish.

4 x 150 g (5 oz) turkey steaks
1 egg
salt and pepper
40–50 g (1½–2 oz) dry breadcrumbs
50 g (2 oz) butter
2 tablespoons oil
To garnish:
12 anchovy fillets
1 hard-boiled egg
1 teaspoon capers

Put the turkey steaks on a board and beat them with a rolling pin as thin as possible. Beat the egg with salt and pepper, then dip the steaks into the beaten egg before coating them with breadcrumbs.

Melt the butter with the oil in a frying pan and fry the crumbed turkey for 5 minutes on each side. Transfer the turkey escalopes to a warmed serving platter. Garnish with a trellis of anchovy fillets, sieved hard-boiled egg (the white separated from the yolk) and capers.

Serves 4

*right: viennese turkey escalopes;
turkey and gammon pie*

Curried Turkey

50 g (2 oz) butter

2 tablespoons hot curry powder

2 onions, chopped

2 garlic cloves, crushed

750 g (1½ lb) cooked turkey meat, finely diced

600 ml (1 pint) turkey or chicken stock

1 tablespoon tomato purée

1 tablespoon sugar

juice of 1 lemon

2 bay leaves

1 thyme sprig

salt and pepper

Melt the butter in a saucepan. Add the curry powder, onions and garlic and fry until softened. Add the turkey and stir in the stock, tomato purée, sugar, lemon juice, salt and pepper and the herbs. Cover and simmer for 1 hour.

If the curry is not hot enough, fry some more curry powder in butter in a separate pan and add it to the turkey mixture. Remove the bay leaf before serving and serve with boiled rice and mango chutney.

Serves 4

Fricassée of Turkey

50 g (2 oz) butter

1 onion, finely chopped

750 g (1½ lb) turkey pieces

40 g (1½ oz) plain flour

600 ml (1 pint) turkey or chicken stock

250 g (8 oz) mushrooms, sliced

1 teaspoon dried tarragon

150 ml (¼ pint) double cream

salt and pepper

chopped parsley, to garnish

Melt the butter in a saucepan. Add the onion and turkey pieces and fry until the turkey pieces are lightly browned. Sprinkle the flour into the pan and cook, stirring, for 1 minute. Stir in the stock and stir until it thickens. Add the mushrooms, tarragon and salt and pepper. Cover and simmer very gently, stirring from time to time, for 1½ hours.

Transfer the turkey pieces to a warmed serving dish and keep hot. Stir the cream into the casserole, adjust the seasoning, if necessary and pour the sauce over the turkey. Sprinkle with chopped parsley and serve.

Serves 4

above: curried turkey
right: turkey croquettes

Turkey Croquettes

500 g (1 lb) cooked turkey meat, minced
1 onion, minced or grated
1 teaspoon dried tarragon
15 g (½ oz) butter, melted
75 g (3 oz) cooked ham, minced
2 eggs, beaten
40–50 g (1½–2 oz) dried breadcrumbs
salt and pepper
oil, for deep frying

Mix together the turkey, onion, tarragon, melted butter, ham, salt and pepper and beaten eggs. Shape into 8 croquettes. Dip them in the remaining beaten egg, then coat with the breadcrumbs.

Deep-fry the croquettes in oil heated to 180–190°C (350–375°F), Gas Mark 4–5 for 7–8 minutes until golden brown. Drain on kitchen paper and serve the croquettes hot.

Makes 8

Roast Poussins

4 x 375 g (12 oz) poussins
50 g (2 oz) butter, melted
plain flour, for dredging
salt and pepper
watercress sprigs, to garnish

Truss the poussins then brush them all over with melted butter and season with salt and pepper. Dredge lightly with flour and roast in a preheated oven, 200°C (400°F), Gas Mark 6, for about 25 minutes until cooked, tender and golden brown. Serve garnished with watercress.

Serves 4

Variation:

Make a marinade for the poussins by whisking together the rind and juice of 4 lemons, 4 cm (1½ inch) piece of fresh root ginger, grated, 6 tablespoons clear honey, 125 ml (4 fl oz) olive oil, 1 lemon grass stalk, split, and salt and pepper to taste. Leave the poussins to marinate in a cool place for at least 12 hours, turning occasionally.

Poussins with Mushroom Sauce

50 g (2 oz) butter
2 x 500 g (1 lb) poussins, halved
2 teaspoons chopped tarragon
75 g (3 oz) mushrooms, sliced
150 ml (¼ pint) chicken stock
2 teaspoons arrowroot
1½ tablespoons water
2 tablespoons double cream
1 tablespoon chopped parsley
salt and pepper

Melt the butter in a sauté or frying pan and brown the poussin halves lightly all over. Season with a little salt and pepper and add the chopped tarragon. Stir in the sliced mushrooms and chicken stock, then bring to the boil. Cover the pan, reduce the heat and simmer gently for about 30 minutes until the poussin halves are cooked and tender.

Transfer the poussin halves to a warmed serving dish and keep hot. Dissolve the arrowroot in the water and stir into the pan. Simmer, stirring, until thickened. Stir in the double cream, then taste and adjust the seasoning, if necessary.

Pour the cream and mushroom sauce over the poussin halves, sprinkle with the chopped parsley and serve.

Serves 4

left: roast poussins
above: poussins with mushroom sauce

Duck and Game

Roast Duck

1 x 1.75–2 kg (3½–4 lb) duck
salt and pepper

Put the duck on a rack in a roasting tin. Prick the skin of the bird all over with a sharp skewer, then rub with salt and pepper. Roast in a preheated oven, 200°C (400°F), Gas Mark 6, for about 1¼ hours until cooked. There is no need to baste the bird during cooking.

Serves 4

Roast Duck with Orange Stuffing

1 x 1.75–2 kg (3½–4 lb) duck
orange wedges, to garnish
Orange Stuffing:
125 g (4 oz) fresh white
   breadcrumbs
duck liver, minced
juice and grated rind of 1 orange
½ teaspoon dried sage
1 shallot, finely chopped
1 small egg, beaten
salt and pepper

To make the stuffing, mix all the ingredients together with salt and pepper to taste, and stuff the duck at the neck. Tuck the neck flap well under the bird and sew or skewer into place. Prick the skin all over with a sharp skewer or a fork.

Place the duck on a rack in a roasting tin. Roast in a preheated oven, 200°C (400°F), Gas Mark 6, for 1½ hours until cooked. Serve garnished with orange wedges.

Serves 4

Duck with Grapefruit

1 x 2 kg (4 lb) duck
1 large grapefruit
salt and pepper

Put the duck on a rack in a roasting tin. Prick the skin all over with a skewer or fork and rub the skin with salt and pepper.

Roast in a preheated oven, 200°C (400°F), Gas Mark 6, for 1 hour 20 minutes until cooked.

Meanwhile, remove the rind from half the grapefruit, being careful not to take any of the white pith with the rind. Cut the rind into thin slivers and blanch in boiling water for 3 minutes, then drain. Peel the grapefruit, removing all the white pith, and separate into segments.

When the duck is cooked, joint it and keep hot on a warmed serving platter. Pour off most of the fat and juices from the roasting tin and put the roasting tin over a low heat on top of the stove. Add the grapefruit segments and rind and heat through gently.

To serve, arrange the grapefruit segments around the duck and pour the pan juices over.

Serves 4

left: roast duck
below: duck with grapefruit

Duck with Grapes

The sauce for this dish is thin and delicate in flavour.

1 x 2 kg (4 lb) duck
300 ml (½ pint) pure grape juice
250 g (8 oz) seedless green grapes, halved
salt and pepper

Put the duck on a rack in a roasting tin. Prick the skin all over with a sharp skewer and rub thoroughly with salt and pepper.

Roast in a preheated oven, 200°C (400°F), Gas Mark 6, for 1 hour 20 minutes until cooked. After 1 hour, pour off most of the fat and juices from the tin and baste the bird with the grape juice.

When the duck is cooked, joint it and arrange on a warmed serving platter. Keep hot.

Skim the fat from the roasting tin. Put the tin over a low heat on top of the stove. Add the grapes and heat through gently. Pour the grape sauce over the duck and serve.

Serves 4

Duck with Lemon

1 x 2 kg (4 lb) duck

2 lemons

50 g (2 oz) sugar

2 tablespoons water

4 tablespoons gin

watercress sprigs, to garnish

salt and pepper

Put the duck on a rack in a roasting tin. Prick the skin all over and rub with salt and pepper.

Roast in a preheated oven, 200°C (400°F), Gas Mark 6, for 1 hour 20 minutes until cooked.

Meanwhile, remove the rind from 1 lemon, being careful not to take any white pith with the rind. Cut the rind into thin slivers. Peel both lemons, removing all the white pith, and separate into segments.

Put the sugar and water into a pan and stir over a low heat to dissolve the sugar. Bring to the boil and boil until golden brown. Remove from the heat and add the lemon segments and rind.

When the duck is cooked, joint it and place on a warmed serving dish. Surround with the caramelized lemon segments and keep hot.

Pour off most of the fat and juices from the roasting tin and place over a low heat on top of the stove. Add the lemon rind mixture and the gin and heat through gently. Pour over the duck and garnish with watercress sprigs.

Serves 4

Cook's Tip: If lemon gin is available, use it instead of ordinary gin.

73

Duck with Orange

1 x 2 kg (4 lb) duck
salt and pepper
300 ml (½ pint) unsweetened orange juice
4 small oranges
4 tablespoons orange-flavoured liqueur

Put the duck on a rack in a roasting tin and prick the skin all over. Rub with salt and pepper. Roast in a preheated oven, 200°C (400°F), Gas Mark 6, for 1 hour 20 minutes. After 1 hour, pour off almost all the fat and juices from the tin and baste the bird with the orange juice then return to the oven.

Remove the rind from 2 oranges, being careful not to take any of the white pith with the rind. Cut the rind into thin slivers and blanch in boiling water for 3 minutes. Drain. Peel all the oranges, removing the white pith, and separate into segments.

When the duck is cooked, joint it and keep hot on a warmed serving platter. Place the pan over a low heat on top of the stove and add the orange segments and shredded rind. Heat through gently.

Arrange the orange segments around the duck. Stir the liqueur into the pan and then pour this sauce over the duck.

Serves 4

Duck with Cherries

1 x 2 kg (4 lb) duck
500 g (1 lb) can Morello cherries
4 tablespoons kirsch
salt and pepper

Put the duck on a rack in a roasting tin. Prick the skin all over and rub with salt and pepper.

Roast in a preheated oven, 200°C (400°F), Gas Mark 6, for 1 hour 20 minutes. After 1 hour, pour off most of the fat and juices from the tin and continue to roast, basting the duck every 10 minutes with the syrup from the can of cherries.

When the duck is cooked, joint it and keep hot on a warmed serving platter. Put the roasting tin over a low heat on top of the stove and add the cherries. Heat through gently, shaking the tin occasionally.

Garnish the duck with the hot cherries. Stir the kirsch into the tin, then pour this sauce over the duck and serve.

Serves 4

above: duck with cherries
right: duck with orange; rouennaise duck

Rouennaise Duck

2 x 1.5 kg (3 lb) ducks with giblets

1 onion, quartered

2 carrots, halved

2 celery sticks, roughly chopped

2 bay leaves

1 tablespoon tomato purée

300 ml (½ pint) dry red wine

40 g (1½ oz) butter

25 g (1 oz) plain flour

100 ml (3½ fl oz) port

salt and pepper

Put the duck giblets (reserving the liver), onion, carrots, celery, bay leaves, tomato purée, wine and 300 ml (½ pint) water in a saucepan and bring to the boil. Simmer for 1 hour, skimming when necessary. Season with salt and pepper. Strain the stock and set aside for the sauce.

Meanwhile, put the ducks on a rack in a roasting tin and prick the skin all over. Roast in a preheated oven, 220°C (425°F), Gas Mark 7, for 45 minutes. Remove from the oven and cut off the legs. Keep the rest of the duck warm. Score the legs and finish cooking them under a preheated grill for 20 minutes.

Melt the butter in a saucepan and add the flour. Cook, stirring, for 1 minute, then stir in the stock. Simmer, stirring, until thickened. Put the sauce in a blender with the liver and port. Blend until smooth. Adjust the seasoning, if necessary. Return to the pan and heat gently until hot.

Slice the duck breasts thinly. Serve a leg and some of the breast to each guest with the sauce in a separate serving bowl.

Serves 4

Roast Goose

1 x 5.5 kg (12 lb) goose
salt and pepper

Take the fat from the body of the goose and spread it over the breast. Place the goose in a roasting tin. Season with salt and pepper and cover loosely with a sheet of foil. Roast in a preheated oven, 200°C (400°F), Gas Mark 6, for 3¼ hours.

Serves 10

Roast Goose with Herb Stuffing

It is always better to stuff a bird at the neck because the flavour gets into the breast, and the stuffing is more thoroughly cooked.

1 x 5.5 kg (12 lb) goose
herbs, to garnish
Herb Stuffing:
40 g (1½ oz) butter
1 onion, finely chopped
goose liver
375 g (12 oz) fresh white
    breadcrumbs
2 teaspoons chopped sage
2 teaspoons chopped mixed herbs
125 g (4 oz) chopped suet
2 eggs, beaten
goose or chicken stock
salt and pepper

To make the stuffing, melt the butter in a frying pan and add the onion and goose liver. Cook gently until the onion is soft but not brown and the liver is lightly

browned on both sides. Remove from the heat and chop the liver. Mix together the remaining stuffing ingredients with the onion and liver and stock to moisten. Season with salt and pepper.

Stuff the neck end of the goose. Pull the neck flap well under the body of the bird and either sew or skewer it. Place in a roasting tin. Cover loosely with a sheet of foil and roast in a preheated oven, 200°C (400°F), Gas Mark 6, for 3¾ hours. Garnish the serving platter with a bunch of herbs.

Serves 10–12

left: roast goose with herb stuffing
above: roast pigeons

Roast Pigeons

4 young pigeons
4 rashers streaky bacon
125 g (4 oz) butter
4 tablespoons port
salt and pepper
**braised red cabbage, to serve
  (optional)**

Truss the birds with fine string and tie a rasher of bacon over each breast. Melt the butter in a roasting tin, add the pigeons and brown lightly on all sides. Season with salt and pepper and roast in a preheated oven, 220°C (425°F), Gas Mark 7, for 30 minutes, basting from time to time. At the last basting pour over the port. Serve the birds with the juices from the tin poured over, and accompanied by braised red cabbage, if liked.

Serves 4

Cook's Tip: To make braised red cabbage, heat 2 tablespoons oil in a heavy casserole and soften 1 onion, diced. Add 500 g (1 lb) red cabbage, finely shredded and 1 large apple, cored and diced. Toss together, then stir in 3 tablespoons red wine vinegar, ¼ teaspoon ground cardamom, 2–3 tablespoons redcurrant jelly and salt and pepper. Cover and cook in a preheated oven, 150°C (300°F), Gas Mark 2, for about 2 hours. Adjust the seasoning, if necessary.

Casserole of Pigeon

40 g (1½ oz) butter

2 large pigeons, halved

125 g (4 oz) streaky bacon, finely diced

2 onions, chopped

1 garlic clove, crushed

40 g (1½ oz) plain flour

300 ml (1½ pint) game or chicken stock

150 ml (¼ pint) red wine

125 g (4 oz) mushrooms, sliced

1 bay leaf

salt and pepper

4 thick slices of bread, toasted, to serve (optional)

Melt the butter in a flameproof casserole, add the pigeon halves, bacon, onions and garlic and fry until well coloured. Sprinkle over the flour, mix in well, then stir in the stock and wine. Add the mushrooms, bay leaf and season to taste with salt and pepper. Bring to the boil, cover, reduce the heat and simmer for about 1½ hours until tender.

Remove the bay leaf, taste and adjust the seasoning, if necessary. Serve on the toast, if using, and pour over the sauce.

Serves 4

right: pigeon and steak pie, casserole of pigeon

Pigeon and Steak Pie

50 g (2 oz) butter

2 large pigeons, jointed

250 g (8 oz) beef skirt, trimmed and finely diced

40 g (1½ oz) plain flour

450 ml (¾ pint) brown ale

1 tablespoon tomato purée

1 teaspoon dried tarragon

1 bay leaf

1 teaspoon Worcestershire sauce

1 small onion, finely chopped

6 mushrooms, sliced

4 rashers streaky bacon, diced

250 g (8 oz) puff pastry, defrosted, if frozen

1 egg, beaten

salt and pepper

Melt the butter in a saucepan and add the pigeon joints and beef. Fry until lightly coloured. Sprinkle over the flour and cook, stirring, for 1 minute. Stir in the brown ale and

bring to the boil. Stir in the tomato purée, tarragon, bay leaf and Worcestershire sauce. Season with salt and pepper. Bring back to the boil, cover the pan, reduce the heat and simmer for about 2 hours or until tender. Remove the bay leaf and allow to cool.

When cold, turn the pigeon mixture into a pie dish. Stir in the onion, mushrooms and bacon. Roll out the puff pastry on a lightly floured surface and use to cover the top of the dish. Make a hole in the centre to allow the steam to escape during cooking. Trim the edges with a knife and flute to seal and decorate. Reroll the pastry trimmings and cut into leaves. Attach to the pie with a little beaten egg. Brush the top of the pie with more egg and bake in a preheated oven, 200°C (400°F), Gas Mark 6, for about 40 minutes until the pastry is crisp and golden.

Serves 4

Pigeon Breasts with Cream Sauce

4 young pigeons
2 onions, chopped
6 mushrooms, sliced
1 thyme sprig
1 tarragon sprig
150 ml (¼ pint) red wine
600 ml (1 pint) game or chicken stock
250 ml (8 fl oz) double cream
4 slices bread, toasted and halved
salt and pepper
parsley sprigs, to garnish

Cut the breasts from the pigeons and put aside. Put the pigeon carcasses into a saucepan, add the onions, mushrooms, herbs, wine and stock and bring to the boil. Cover the pan and simmer for about 1 hour.

Put the pigeon breasts into another saucepan and strain over the stock mixture. Poach for about 30 minutes until tender. Remove the pigeon breasts from the pan and keep hot. Reduce the cooking stock by boiling briskly until 300 ml (½ pint) is left. Season with salt and pepper to taste and whisk in the cream. Arrange the pigeon breasts on the toast and pour over the sauce. Garnish with parsley sprigs.

Serves 4

Roast Guinea Fowl

Guinea fowl are lean, with fine-textured flesh and a delicate gamey flavour.

1 x 1.5 kg (3 lb) guinea fowl
3 rashers streaky bacon
50 g (2 oz) butter
salt and pepper
Mushroom Sauce:
65 g (2½ oz) unsalted butter, diced
175 g (6 oz) mixed mushrooms, (eg. oyster, shiitake, brown cap), sliced
300 ml (½ pint) red wine
450 ml (¾ pint) chicken stock

Truss the guinea fowl and tie the bacon over the breast with fine string. Melt the butter in a roasting tin, add the guinea fowl and brown on all sides, for about 10 minutes. Season the bird with salt and pepper and roast in a preheated oven, 200°C (400°F), Gas Mark 6, for about 1 hour, basting frequently.

Meanwhile, make the sauce. Heat 20 g (¾ oz) of the butter in a large frying pan. Add the mushrooms and cook, stirring, for 3–4 minutes. Remove with a slotted spoon. Add the wine and stock to the pan, bring to the boil and simmer for 15 minutes until reduced by half. Whisk in the remaining butter, add the mushrooms and season to taste. Serve with the guinea fowl.

Serves 4

Roast Grouse

Grouse have a powerful gamey flavour and are in season from August 12th to December 10th.

4 rashers streaky bacon
2 large or 4 small young grouse
50 g (2 oz) butter
100 ml (3½ fl oz) red wine
4 thick slices bread, toasted
watercress sprigs, to garnish
To serve (optional):
redcurrant jelly
bread sauce

Carefully tie the bacon rashers on to the breasts of the birds and truss the birds with fine string. Melt the butter in a roasting tin, add the grouse and fry until they have a good colour. Transfer to a preheated oven, 200 C, (400 F) Gas Mark 6, and roast for 30–45 minutes, depending on the size of the bird.

About 10 minutes before the grouse are cooked, baste them with the wine. Arrange on the toast with the pan juices poured over. Garnish with watercress sprigs and serve with redcurrant jelly and bread sauce, if liked.

Serves 4

Casserole of Grouse

50 g (2 oz) butter
2 grouse, jointed
125 g (4 oz) gammon, diced
4 onions, chopped
40 g (1½ oz) plain flour
200 ml (7 fl oz) red wine
300 ml (½ pint) game or chicken stock
10 mushrooms, sliced
1 bay leaf
salt and pepper

Melt the butter in a flameproof casserole and fry the grouse, gammon and onions until lightly browned. Sprinkle over the flour and cook, stirring, for 1 minute. Stir in the wine and stock and bring to the boil. Add the mushrooms and bay leaf and season with salt and pepper. Bring to the boil again, reduce the heat, cover the casserole and simmer for about 2 hours until the grouse is tender. Remove the bay leaf and serve.

Serves 4

right: casserole of grouse, roast grouse

Roast Partridges

4 rashers streaky bacon
4 young partridges
50 g (2 oz) butter
125 ml (4 fl oz) red wine
salt and pepper
4 thick slices of bread, toasted
watercress sprigs, to garnish

Tie the bacon across the breasts of the partridges and truss the birds with fine string. Melt the butter in a roasting tin and brown the birds on all sides. Transfer to a preheated oven, 200°C (400°F), Gas Mark 6, and roast for 30–40 minutes.

After 20 minutes, baste with the wine and season with salt and pepper. Continue to baste at intervals. Serve on the toast with the pan juices poured over and garnish with the watercress sprigs.

Serves 4

Roast Pheasant

2 rashers streaky bacon
1 x 1.5 kg (3 lb) pheasant
50 g (2 oz) butter
150 ml (¼ pint) red wine
salt and pepper
watercress sprigs, to garnish
To serve (optional):
potato crisps
bacon rolls

Tie the bacon across the breast of the pheasant with fine string and truss the bird. Melt the butter in a roasting tin and fry the pheasant on all sides until light brown. Season with salt and pepper and roast in a preheated oven, 220°C (425°F), Gas Mark 7, for 1 hour 20 minutes. After 1 hour, baste with the wine.

To serve, remove the legs for 2 portions and carve 2 more from the breasts. Serve the juices as gravy. Serve with potato crisps and bacon rolls, if liked, and garnish with watercress sprigs.

Serves 4

left: roast pheasant
above: normandy pheasant

Normandy Pheasant

50g (2 oz) butter
3 cooking apples, peeled, cored and
  finely chopped
2 tablespoons lemon juice
4 pheasant breasts
3 tablespoons double cream
salt and pepper
watercress sprigs, to garnish

Melt 25 g (1 oz) of the butter in a frying pan. Add the apples and lemon juice and fry gently until softened. Add two-thirds of the apple to a casserole dish that will accommodate the apples and pheasant breasts.

Fry the pheasant breasts in the remaining butter and place them on top of the apples. Season with salt and pepper and add the remaining apple. Sprinkle over the cream. Cover the casserole and cook in a preheated oven, 200°C (400°F), Gas Mark 6, for 20–40 minutes until the pheasant is tender. The apples and cream should form a delicious sauce. Serve garnished with watercress sprigs.

Serves 4

Special Occasions

Chicken in Spicy Apricot Sauce

Fresh apricots may be used in season in place of canned ones, but they must be sweetened. Place 500 g (1 lb) fresh apricot halves in a pan with 300 ml (½ pint) water and 2 tablespoons sugar. Poach gently until tender, and then remove the apricots and reduce the liquid by boiling to 150 ml (¼ pint).

1 x 2 kg (4 lb) chicken, skinned and jointed
50 ml (2 fl oz) oil
2 large onions, finely chopped
2 garlic cloves, crushed
2 tablespoons ground coriander
1 teaspoon ground cardamom
1½ teaspoons chilli powder
1 teaspoon sugar
425 g (14 oz) can plum tomatoes, drained and chopped
425 g (14 oz) can apricots, drained and half the liquid reserved
salt

Place the chicken joints in a large ovenproof casserole. Mix together the remaining ingredients in a bowl, adding half the apricots. Pour the mixture evenly over the chicken. Cover and bake in a preheated oven, 180°C (350°F), Gas Mark 4, for 1 hour.

Remove the casserole from the oven and gently spoon the sauce over the chicken pieces. Arrange the remaining fruit attractively on top of the chicken, then cover and cook for a further 30 minutes until the chicken is tender. Serve hot.

Serves 4

Chicken in Coconut Milk

Galangal is sold in some supermarkets. If unavailable, use the same amount of fresh root ginger.

1 x 1.5 kg (3 lb) chicken, cut into 8 pieces
900 ml (1½ pints) coconut milk
5 cm (2 inch) piece of galangal, peeled and finely chopped
3 green chillies, deseeded and finely chopped
8 coriander sprigs, stems finely chopped
4 kaffir lime leaves (optional)
4 black peppercorns, crushed
1 teaspoon grated lime rind
2 tablespoons fish sauce (*nam pla*)
1 tablespoon lime juice
salt
coriander leaves, to garnish

Skin the chicken and place in a pan. Skim off the coconut cream from the milk and reserve. Pour the remaining coconut milk over the chicken. Add the galangal, chillies, coriander, lime leaves, if using, the crushed peppercorns and lime rind and season with salt.

Bring to the boil, then reduce the heat and simmer gently, uncovered, for 35–40 minutes until the chicken is tender and half of the liquid has evaporated.

About 5 minutes before serving, pour in the reserved coconut cream and bring to the boil. Add the fish sauce and lime juice. Transfer to a warmed serving dish and sprinkle with coriander leaves, to garnish.

Serves 4

Cook's Tip: Galangal is a member of the ginger family. It resembles ginger in appearance but has a smoother skin that has a shiny, pink tinge. The flower is more delicate and earthy than ginger.

right: thai chicken curry

Thai Chicken Curry

5 cm (2 inch) piece of fresh root
  ginger, peeled and chopped
40 g (1½ oz) coriander leaves,
  chopped
2–4 green chillies, chopped
4 garlic cloves
2 onions, quartered
1 tablespoon plain flour
1 teaspoon chilli powder
8 chicken thighs, skinned

3 tablespoons oil
300 ml (½ pint) water
50 g (2 oz) creamed coconut
juice of 1 lemon
salt
lemon twists, to garnish

Place the ginger, coriander, chillies, garlic and onions in a blender or food processor and purée.

Mix the flour, salt and chilli powder together and use to coat the chicken. Heat the oil, add the chicken and fry, turning occasionally, until golden all over.

Remove and keep warm.

Add the spice paste to the pan and fry, stirring, for 5 minutes. Stir in the water, then return the chicken to the pan. Cover and simmer gently for 25 minutes.

Stir in the coconut and the lemon juice, then cover and simmer for 10 minutes. Serve immediately, garnished with lemon twists.

Serves 4

Chicken with Yogurt

50 g (2 oz) butter
1 x 1.5 kg (3 lb) chicken, jointed
1 onion, chopped
½ green pepper, cored, deseeded and
    chopped
1 garlic clove, crushed
65 g (2½ oz) plain flour
600 ml (1 pint) chicken stock
300 ml (½ pint) natural yogurt
salt and pepper
chopped chervil or parsley, to garnish

Melt the butter in a flameproof casserole. Add the chicken pieces, onion, green pepper and garlic and fry until the chicken pieces are lightly browned on all sides. Sprinkle the flour over and cook, stirring, for 1 minute. Stir in the chicken stock and season with salt and pepper to taste. Bring to the boil and simmer for 30 minutes.

Stir in the yogurt and continue cooking very gently, covered, for a further 30 minutes. Taste and adjust the seasoning, if necessary and serve, garnished with chopped chervil or parsley. Plain boiled rice makes a good accompaniment to this dish.

Serves 4

Chicken with Black Truffle

2 small or 1 medium black truffle(s),
  thinly sliced
125 ml (4 fl oz) Madeira wine
1 x 1.75 kg (3½ lb) chicken
175 g (6 oz) liver pâté
125 g (4 oz) fresh white breadcrumbs
125 g (4 oz) butter
salt and pepper

Marinate the truffle in the Madeira
wine for 1 hour. Lift the skin on the
chicken breasts by inserting your
fingers at the neck end and gently
easing the skin away from the flesh.
Insert the truffle slices under the
skin of the chicken and secure the
skin firmly under the body. Mix
together the Madeira, pâté and
breadcrumbs, with salt and pepper
to taste. Stuff the body of the
chicken with the mixture, and truss.

Melt the butter in a roasting tin
or flameproof casserole. Add the
chicken and brown all over. Cover
and transfer to a preheated oven,
200°C (400°F), Gas Mark 6 and cook
for 30 minutes, then reduce the
heat to 180°C (350°F), Gas Mark 4.
Continue cooking, basting
frequently, for 1 hour until the
chicken is golden and tender.

Transfer the chicken to a warmed
serving platter and pour over the
pan juices. Carve at the table. Serve
with seasonal vegetables.

Serves 4

Chicken in White Wine

50 g (2 oz) butter
1 x 1.5 kg (3 lb) chicken, quartered,
  or 4 chicken portions
25 g (1 oz) plain flour
300 ml (½ pint) dry white wine
300 ml (½ pint) chicken stock
2 bay leaves
1 thyme sprig
salt and pepper
watercress sprigs, to garnish

Melt the butter in a flameproof
casserole. Season the chicken pieces
with salt and pepper and fry until
lightly browned on all sides.
Sprinkle the flour into the casserole
and cook, stirring, for 2 minutes.

Pour over the wine and stock and
stir well. Bring to the boil and skim.
Add salt and pepper, the bay leaves
and thyme. Cover and simmer
gently for 1 hour. Remove the bay
leaves and adjust the seasoning, if
necessary, before serving, garnished
with watercress sprigs.

Serves 4

left: chicken with yogurt
above: chicken in white wine

Chicken Argenteuil

75 g (3 oz) butter

1 x 1.5 kg (3 lb) chicken, skinned and
  quartered, or 4 chicken portions

50 g (2 oz) plain flour

600 ml (1 pint) chicken stock

150 ml (¼ pint) water

500 g (1 lb) fresh asparagus tips

2 tablespoons double cream

salt and pepper

Melt 25 g (1 oz) of the butter in a saucepan. Add the chicken pieces and fry until lightly browned on all sides. Sprinkle 25 g (1 oz) of the flour into the pan and cook, stirring, for 1 minute. Stir in the stock, then bring to the boil and skim. Season with salt and pepper.

Cover the pan and simmer gently for 1 hour. Transfer the chicken pieces to a warmed serving dish and keep hot.

Bring the water to the boil in a saucepan and add a pinch of salt.

Add the asparagus tips and poach until just tender. Strain the cooking water into the sauce. Keep the asparagus tips hot.

Mix the remaining butter and flour together to make a paste. Add in small pieces to the sauce and cook, stirring, until thickened. Stir in the cream. Adjust the seasoning, if necessary.

Pour the sauce over the chicken and garnish with the asparagus tips.

Serves 4

Chicken Marengo

125 g (4 oz) butter

1 x 1.75 kg (3½ lb) chicken, quartered, or 4 chicken portions

6 shallots

2 garlic cloves, crushed

125 g (4 oz) plain flour

6 tomatoes, skinned and quartered

175 g (6 oz) button mushrooms

1 bay leaf

1 teaspoon dried oregano

1 white truffle, chopped, but kept in its juice (optional)

1 bottle of Marsala

100 ml (3½ fl oz) brandy

salt and pepper

Melt 75 g (3 oz) of the butter in a flameproof casserole. Add the chicken pieces, shallots and garlic and fry until the chicken is lightly browned on all sides. Sprinkle over 50 g (2 oz) of the flour and cook, stirring, for 1 minute. Add the tomatoes, mushrooms, bay leaf, oregano, truffle with its juice, if using, and Marsala. Bring to the boil and skim. Cover the casserole and simmer for 1¼ hours until the chicken is tender.

About 10 minutes before the chicken is ready, add the brandy and stir well. Mix together the remaining butter and flour to make a paste. Add in small pieces to the sauce, stirring, and simmer until thickened. Remove the bay leaf and taste and adjust the seasoning, if necessary, before serving.

Serves 4

Tarragon Chaudfroid of Chicken

1 x 1.75 kg (3½ lb) chicken

1 bunch of tarragon

25 g (1 oz) butter, melted

2 egg yolks

juice of 1½ lemons

1 teaspoon sugar

300 ml (½ pint) olive oil

70 g (2½ oz) packet aspic jelly powder

450 ml (¾ pint) water

salt and pepper

Season the chicken with salt and pepper, and stuff the body with the tarragon, reserving a few sprigs for the garnish. Truss the chicken and brush with the melted butter. Place in a roasting pan and roast in a preheated oven, 200°C (400°F), Gas Mark 6, for 1 hour 20 minutes. Set aside to cool.

Meanwhile, make a mayonnaise with the egg yolks, lemon juice, sugar, a little salt and pepper and the olive oil (see page 56).

Make up the aspic with the water, according to the packet. (This quantity of water will produce a stiffer aspic than usual.) Allow the jelly to cool, almost to setting point.

Skin the chicken and cut into attractive serving pieces, i.e. 2 breast pieces, 2 thigh pieces, and 2 wings. Beat all but 4 tablespoons of the aspic into the mayonnaise and use to coat the chicken pieces. Chill in the refrigerator until set.

Blanch the remaining tarragon in boiling water for 2 minutes, then refresh in cold water. Garnish the chicken with the blanched tarragon, and glaze with the reserved aspic. Chill again until set.

Serves 4

Roast Chicken with Braised Celeriac

1 x 1.5 kg (3 lb) chicken
50 g (2 oz) melted butter
1 large celeriac bulb, cut into
    matchsticks
juice of ½ lemon
40 g (1½ oz) butter
50 g (2 oz) can anchovy fillets
salt and pepper
parsley sprigs, to garnish

Truss the chicken and season with salt and pepper. Brush with the melted butter and place in a roasting tin. Roast in a preheated oven, 200°C (400°F), Gas Mark 6, for 1¼ hours, basting once or twice with the melted butter.

Meanwhile, blanch the celeriac for 4 minutes in boiling salted water with the lemon juice. Drain well.

Remove the chicken from the oven and keep hot on a warmed dish. Add the celeriac to the roasting tin with the butter. Mix well with the pan juices. Add the anchovies with their oil. Cover with foil and cook gently on top of the stove until the celeriac has softened.

Carve the chicken and arrange on a warmed serving dish. Surround with the celeriac mixture. Garnish with parsley sprigs.

Serves 4

Chicken in Plum Sauce

500 g (1 lb) plums, pitted
50 g (2 oz) butter
1 x 1.5 kg (3 lb) chicken, jointed
1 onion, chopped
juice of ½ lemon
1 bay leaf
salt and pepper

Put the plums in a pan, add a little water, then cover and simmer gently until the plums are tender, cool slightly, then purée in a blender, or press through a sieve. Set aside.

Melt the butter in a flameproof casserole. Add the chicken and onion and fry gently until the chicken is lightly browned on all sides. Add the plum purée, lemon juice, bay leaf and salt and pepper.

Cover and transfer to a preheated oven, 180°C (350°F), Gas Mark 4. Cook for 1½ hours until tender. Remove the bay leaf and adjust the seasoning, if necessary, before serving.

Serves 4

above: chicken with grapefruit, chicken with fresh pineapple

Chicken with Grapefruit

50 g (2 oz) butter
1 x 1.5 kg (3 lb) chicken
2 shallots, chopped
1–2 grapefruit, according to size
1 tablespoon sugar
salt and pepper

Melt the butter in a roasting tin and add the chicken and shallots. Fry until lightly browned, then season with salt and pepper. Transfer to a preheated oven, 200°C (400°F), Gas Mark 6 and roast for 1¼ hours.

Meanwhile, peel the rind from the grapefruit, being careful not to take any of the white pith with the rind, and cut it into very thin

Chicken with Fresh Pineapple

1 x 1.75 kg (3½ lb) chicken
1 pineapple, peeled, cored and thinly
   sliced
50 g (2 oz) butter
2 shallots, chopped
salt and pepper
watercress sprigs, to garnish

Lift the skin on the breast of the
chicken by inserting your fingers
from the neck end and gently
easing the skin away from the flesh.
Put a slice of pineapple under the
skin on each breast of the chicken.

Melt the butter in a roasting tin
and add the shallots. Cook until
softened. Add the chicken and
brown lightly on all sides. Season
with salt and pepper, then transfer
to a preheated oven, 200°C (400°F),
Gas Mark 6 and roast for 1 hour
20 minutes.

Transfer the chicken to a warm
serving platter and keep hot. Add
the remaining pineapple slices to
the roasting tin and cook on top of
the stove until the pineapple is
heated through. Arrange around
the chicken and garnish with
watercress sprigs.

Serves 4

shreds. Blanch in boiling water for
3 minutes, then drain. Remove the
pith from the grapefruit, then
separate into segments. Peel the
segments, if possible. Sprinkle with
the sugar.

Transfer the chicken to a warm
serving platter and keep hot. Pour
the fat from the roasting tin, then
put the tin over the heat, on top of
the stove. Stir in the grapefruit and
the shredded rind. Heat through
gently. Serve the grapefruit mixture
with the chicken.

Serves 4

Roast Lemon Poussins

75 g (3 oz) butter, softened
finely grated rind and juice of
  2 lemons
4 x 500 g (1 lb) poussins
4 tablespoons chopped parsley
2 shallots, chopped
4 tablespoons dry white wine
salt and pepper
To garnish:
parsley sprigs
lemon twists

Put the butter, lemon rind and juice in a small bowl and beat until well blended. Spread all over the poussins and inside the cavities. Mix the parsley and shallots together and place a spoonful inside each poussin. Sprinkle with salt and pepper to taste, place in a roasting tin and pour a tablespoon of wine over each poussin.

Roast in a preheated oven, 180°C (350°F), Gas Mark 4, for 30 minutes, basting occasionally. Increase the heat to 200°C (400°F), Gas Mark 6, and cook for a further 10 minutes, until well browned and crisp.

Transfer to a warm serving dish and garnish with parsley and lemon twists. Serve with sauté potatoes and green beans, if liked.

Serves 4

Chestnut Stuffing for Roast Turkey

125 g (4 oz) minced veal
turkey liver, minced
75 g (3 oz) bacon, rind removed and
  minced
grated rind of 1 orange
2 tablespoons chopped parsley
500 g (1 lb) can unsweetened
  chestnut purée
1 egg, beaten
salt and pepper

Mix all the ingredients thoroughly together with salt and pepper to taste. Stuff the neck of the turkey, working the stuffing well under the skin. Fold the flap under the bird and secure it well with a skewer or by sewing. It is important that the stuffing does not come out during cooking.

Makes enough for a 4.5 kg (10 lb) turkey

right: roast turkey and gammon

Roast Turkey and Gammon

1 x 4.5 kg (10 lb) turkey (or whatever
  size you wish)
1 x 1.5–2 kg (3–4 lb) piece of
  gammon bacon (size to fit the
  bird's cavity), soaked in cold water
  overnight
2 bay leaves
50 g (2 oz) butter, softened
salt and pepper
watercress, to garnish

With a sharp knife, separate the rib cage from the flesh of the turkey and, with poultry shears, cut out the rib cage. Cut the bacon roughly to fit inside the bird. Put the bacon in a pan with the bay leaves, cover with cold water and bring to the boil. Cover and simmer for 45 minutes. Remove and set aside to cool.

Strip off the rind and fat and put the bacon inside the turkey, making the best shape you can. Place the turkey in a roasting pan and spread the softened butter all over it. Sprinkle with salt and pepper and cover with foil. Roast in a preheated oven, 160°C (325°F), Gas Mark 3, for 3½–3¾ hours.

If it is difficult to carve the turkey and the bacon at the same time, remove the bacon and slice it separately. Serve garnished with watercress.

Serves 12

Index